W9-BTS-819

The Millennium Meltdown

The Year 2000 Computer Crisis

Grant R. Jeffrey

Frontier Research Publications, Inc.
P.O. Box 129, Station "U", Toronto, Ontario M8Z 5M4

The Millennium Meltdown

Copyright © 1998 by Grant R. Jeffrey

All rights reserved. No part of this book may be reproduced or transmitted in any form or by any means electronic or mechanical, including photocopy, recording, or any information, storage and retrieval system now known or to be invented, without the written permission of the publisher, except for brief quotations by a reviewer for use in a magazine, newspaper, or broadcast.

Library of Congress Cataloging in Publication Data:

Jeffrey, Grant R.
The Millennium Meltdown: The Year 2000 Computer Crisis

1. Eschatology   2. Year 2000 Computer Crisis   3. Finance - Investments
1. Title

July 1998   Frontier Research Publications, Inc.
Third Printing October 1998 – 170,000 books in print

ISBN 0-921714-48-3

Unless otherwise indicated, Scripture quotations are from the Authorized King James Version.

Cover design: The Riordon Design Group
Printed in Canada: Harmony Printing Limited

COMMENTS ON GRANT JEFFREY'S
TEN BEST SELLING BOOKS

ARMAGEDDON	• MESSIAH
APOCALYPSE	• PRINCE OF DARKNESS
FINAL WARNING	• THE SIGNATURE OF GOD
HEAVEN	• THE HANDWRITING OF GOD
FLEE THE DARKNESS	• THE MYSTERIOUS BIBLE CODES

"Grant Jeffrey has written an extraordinary new book, *The Signature of God*, that provides astonishing proof that the Bible was inspired by God. Grant is recognized as the leading researcher in Bible Prophecy today."
Hal Lindsey, Hal Lindsey Ministries

"*Prince of Darkness* was written by acclaimed Bible Prophecy teacher Grant R. Jeffrey. This unequaled masterpiece is the result of 30 years of intense research. It will stir you and inspire you as few books have . . . It is extremely well written — extraordinarily researched and fascinatingly presented . . . this is the best book I have ever read on this subject."
Jack Van Impe, Jack Van Impe Ministries

"Grant Jeffrey... is now a best selling author throughout North America. . . . His breakthrough book was his first, *Armageddon — Appointment With Destiny* . . . Bantam Books later picked it up, and it turned out to be their No. 1 religious best seller in 1990."
Philip Marchand, Book Review Editor, Toronto Star, Aug. 1, 1992

"Grant Jeffrey is one of Canada's most prolific religious authors. The tone of *The Signature of God* is one of deep passion for the truth of the gospel and evangelistic concern for the unbeliever. If you are going to give a gift this year to one who is not yet a believer, this is it."
Dr. Garry E. Milley: President, Eastern Pentecostal Bible College, 1996

"We are excited about Grant Jeffrey's new book . . . Now the book with the latest information on prophetic fulfillment, the book of the nineties, is *Armageddon: Appointment With Destiny*. It will show that God is in control and, most importantly, it will also prove to be a powerful witnessing tool to those who need Christ."
David Mainse: Host, 100 Huntley Street

"*The Signature of God* is highly recommended as a superb resource for sharing and defending one's faith in the skeptical world in which we live."
Craig Stoll, Book Buyer, Mardel Christian Bookstores, 1997

Table of Contents

Acknowledgements

The Millennium Meltdown is the result of over eighteen months of research involving dozens of technical manuals, books, articles, and thousands of pages of Internet material. Additionally, countless hours of Bible study over the last 35 years, and eighteen years as a professional financial planner are reflected in the spiritual and practical strategies suggested in these pages. Although more than a dozen books are listed in the footnotes and selected bibliography, these books represent only a fraction of the authors who have influenced and challenged my thinking.

My parents, Lyle and Florence Jeffrey, instilled in me a profound love for the Lord and His word; they have continually encouraged me in this project.

I would like to dedicate this book to my loving wife, Kaye, who is my faithful partner in ministry and research. She provides me with continual encouragement and inspiration in sharing this research with others.

In addition, I would like to acknowledge the excellent research and editorial work completed by Adrienne Tigchelaar, Nancy Phillips, and Rick Blanchette.

I trust that the information revealed in the following pages will encourage you to complete additional research yourself on the Year 2000 computer crisis. The knowledge you gain from this book should help you to understand the great challenge facing all of us and assist you in making practical preparations to minimize the disruptions to your life and family as we begin the next century.

Grant R. Jeffrey,
Toronto, Ontario
July 1998

Notice from the publisher regarding
The Millennium Meltdown

The Millennium Meltdown offers only general observations based on the author's research, and makes no specific recommendations.

Our intention in this book is to provide Grant Jeffrey's opinions regarding economic and practical implications of the approaching Year 2000 computer crisis. Neither Frontier Research Publications, Inc. nor Grant Jeffrey is able to provide individual advice. Frontier Research and the author are not engaged in rendering legal, accounting, investing, or other professional advice. The reader should seek the services of a qualified professional accountant, lawyer, or financial planner before taking any actions.

The author and the publisher cannot be held responsible for any loss incurred as a result of the application of any of the information in this book. We have endeavored to assure the accuracy of the statistics and information that appear throughout this book. Please remember that *The Millennium Meltdown* is a guide, not a definitive source of investment information. When you have a specific question about your individual situation, check with your accountant, broker, banker, or financial consultant.

1

Introduction:
The Year 2000 Crisis

On December 31, 1999, almost six billion people worldwide will welcome in the new millennium with the greatest New Year's Eve parties ever held in our lifetime. They will celebrate by counting down the final seconds of the last year of this momentous twentieth century, but it is not only the party-goers who will be counting time. Around the world, hundreds of millions of computers will also make the transition from the old year to the new, from the year 1999 to the year 2000. And when they do, many of these engines of modern society will begin to crash or malfunction, precipitating a global crisis, the scope of which we have not experienced since World War II.

At 12:00 A.M., January 1, 2000, beginning in nations near the international dateline (such as Fiji and New Zealand), the world's computers will roll over the digits "99" (1999) to "00" (2000). When they do, modern society will reap the whirlwind sown by an innocent cost-savings decision made by computer programmers in the early days of the computer industry to record computer dates with only two-digit fields instead of four-digit fields (e.g., "73" instead of "1973"). So, what is the problem? With only a two-digit date field, the computers have no means to distinguish the year 2000 from the year 1900.

Information technology specialists have coined this global crisis the "Y2K" crisis or virus. Y2K is an acronym for "year 2000." The Y stands for "year," and 2K indicates "2000," K being an abbreviation for the Latin word "kilo," which means "one thousand." (A "Y2K-compliant" computer has been modified to correctly accept the year 2000; a "Y2K-noncompliant" computer has not.)

Despite years of warnings and ample time to avert the crisis, the lights will go out in many cities around the world. Many government agencies and businesses will be temporarily crippled. And the stock market and banking systems—institutions as critical to modern life as the government itself—will suffer challenges not experienced since the Great Depression. Every aspect of our complex society is vulnerable because sophisticated computers interlink almost every system in our infrastructure. The failure to correct this massive problem before the year-2000 deadline could threaten our jobs, our safety, our food, and our finances. Moreover, many scholars of Bible prophecy believe that this crisis may hasten the creation of the coming world government that was prophesied to arise in the last days, according to the ancient prophets of the Bible.

The Y2K crisis is unique among all of the disasters that have afflicted humanity through the centuries because it is the first catastrophe in history that will arrive precisely on schedule—on January 1, 2000. This appointment with destiny cannot be postponed or avoided. We know precisely when it will begin affecting the vast networks of computer systems that control much of the infrastructure of our modern world. Either we will correct the problem that endangers our computer systems before this approaching deadline arrives, or we will suffer expensive and catastrophic consequences that could affect the life of every citizen in the modern industrial world.

In light of the potential for disaster the Year 2000 crisis poses to our society and to our individual lives, it is essential that we learn how to protect our family, our homes, and our finances. *The Millennium Meltdown* will document the extent of the impending computer collapse, what steps are being taken to remedy the problem, and how this crisis could affect nearly every area of your life in the first few months of the next millennium. In addition, several chapters will outline practical strategies to protect your family from the worst effects of the greatest technological crisis in our lifetime.

How Did This Problem Occur?

In the 1960s and 1970s programmers in the fledgling computer industry made a fateful decision to save memory and space by recording year dates (such as 1948) with only two digits (i.e., "48"). They believed that more-advanced models would replace the older computer systems long before the arrival of the year 2000. No one anticipated that these early computer programs and mainframes would work so well that many government agencies and large corporations would still be using these systems thirty years later. Unfortunately, unless these hundreds of millions of computers are corrected prior to January 1, 2000, when the year "99" (1999) rolls over to "00" (2000), these aging computer systems will misinterpret the new year number field as 1900 instead of 2000.

According to the government's own experts, when this occurs, many of our most essential computer systems may do one of three things: (1) they may shut down or crash; (2) they may begin to produce massive errors and miscalculations; or (3) they may begin to produce small, perhaps undetected errors that may not be apparent for some time. Any of these options may lead to major disasters for government agencies, corporations, and the billions of citizens worldwide who depend on these systems to provide the necessities of modern life.

Dates are found scattered throughout most computer programs. In fact, one of the main functions of computers is to accurately calculate the precise time that has passed between events (e.g., the duration of time from the application of an insurance policy to the date of the first claim). Some experts suggest that within a computer's millions of lines of software code, as many as one line out of twenty may contain date fields. The failure to correctly calculate the date can cause havoc. Security computers could open time-controlled bank vaults at the wrong time, elevators could shut down, or the schedules for planes and trains could be miscalculated, causing accidents and travelling chaos.

As an example of how the Y2K crisis could affect your life, consider the possible problems with a large company's computer system. Imagine that your mother worked for a company until her retirement and that your sister is currently an employee with the same company. In 1999 ("99") the computer would normally calculate the difference between your mother's birth date in 1934 and 1999 as 65 years and send her a well-deserved monthly pension check. Determining that the difference between the year 1999 ("99") and your sister's birthday in 1965 is 34 years, the same computer system would subtract her required monthly pension deduction from her paycheck. However, if the company's computer system is not corrected by the year 2000, it will begin to make expensive errors.

In the year 2000, when the Y2K-noncompliant computer analyzes your mother's age to verify her qualifications for receiving her next monthly pension check, it will miscalculate the difference between "34" and "00" (which it will read as 1900) and assume that she is only thirty-four years old. Consequently, the system may cut off her pension checks. The computer will also miscalculate the difference between your sister's birth date in "65" and "00" (which it reads as 1900) as being 65 years and begin to send her unexpected pension checks.

Another type of problem may occur when computers check the expiration date of a credit card to determine if it is still valid, or an insurance policy to determine if the policy is still in force at the time of a claim. A Y2K-noncompliant computer system will reject your credit card or your insurance claim because it will wrongly conclude that your credit card or policy expired in 1900.

With just a few examples, it is not difficult to see how easily the interlinked information systems that run our modern world could break down. Indeed, if governments and corporations fail to move quickly enough to modify their computers and software code before the year 2000, the results will be catastrophic. Unfortunately, most government agencies and businesses have waited too long to begin these essential repairs. Had every company and agency begun a serious Year 2000 modification effort in 1995 or 1996, most of the nations' essential computers could have been safely corrected by 1998, leaving a whole year for the new systems to be properly tested in 1999 to make sure they were working properly.

I have entitled this book *The Millennium Meltdown* because the Y2K computer crisis has the potential to cause widespread damage to the critical information systems that control our modern society in a manner analogous to how damage is caused by a malfunctioning nuclear reactor, which can lead to a nuclear meltdown. A meltdown occurs when a failure in the safety systems of a nuclear reactor prevents the vital coolant water from cooling down the superheated nuclear core. The continuing nuclear reaction causes the superheated nuclear core to melt down through hundreds of feet of reinforced concrete and metal. When the nuclear fuel rods melt through the power plant's foundation into the ground, they may eventually encounter groundwater deep within the earth. If that happens, the resulting superheated steam can explode and cause deadly radiation to expand at great speed into the atmosphere, contaminating communities for miles around. Just as an out-of-control nuclear reactor can produce a potential meltdown (as occurred at Three Mile Island in Pennsylvania and Chernobyl in the Ukraine), the multiple failures of interlinked computer systems worldwide could cause chaos and damage to our nation, our businesses, and our families.

For eighteen years, I was a professional financial planner in the banking and insurance industry. In addition to completing my Chartered Life Underwriter degree, I spent thousands of hours in extensive studies of financial systems and economics. As a result of my professional experience and the extensive interviews I have conducted with senior government consultants and professionals in the fields of banking, insurance, accounting, transportation, pharmaceuticals, and utilities, I have come to the conclusion that the Y2K problem has the potential to produce severe economic recession for a significant period of time and cause the bankruptcy of numerous businesses. As I document in this book, my research suggests that although the Y2K crisis may only last a short period of time (from a few months to a few years, depending on the country in which you live), it may be devastating for those who are unprepared. My hope is that *The Millennium Meltdown* will alert you to the nature and the extent of the Y2K crisis and provide you with vital information on how you can protect yourself and your family from the worst possible dangers.

How Widespread Is This Year 2000 Problem?

Our world is interconnected in countless ways by complex computer systems that make our lives both convenient and safe. However, our near-total reliance on computers to run everything from traffic lights to home security systems to electric power grids—which are the lifeblood of our nation—makes modern society tremendously vulnerable if these countless computers were to simultaneously experience massive failure.

Newsweek magazine was among the first major media to acknowledge the Year 2000 computer crisis in their June 2, 1997 issue. This pivotal article, provocatively entitled "The Day the World Shut Down," contains a serious analysis of the Year 2000 computer problem, as well as a reasonable account of the dangers to our economy and the government's computer systems that the problem poses. After arresting the reader's attention with such disturbing questions as, "Will power plants shut down and your phone go out? Will your Social Security checks disappear into cyberspace? Will your bank account vanish?" the *Newsweek* article continues with the following analysis:

> Could it really happen? . . . Incredibly, according to computer experts, corporate information officers, congressional leaders and basically anyone who's given the matter a fair hearing, the answer is Yes, Yes, 2,000 Times Yes! Yes—unless we successfully complete the most ambitious and costly technology project in history, one where the payoff comes not in amassing riches or extending Web access, but securing raw survival. . . . In the worst case scenario, the entire financial infrastructure, including the stock market, will go haywire. Balances, records, and transactions will be lost. . . . Y2K could be the event that could all but paralyze the planet.[1]

Senator Fred Thompson asks, "What is the U.S. government doing? Not enough. . . . It's ironic that this administration that prides itself on being so high tech is not really facing up to the potential disaster that is down the road a little bit. . . . If Y2K triggers an economic and government collapse, it may well be the vice president who suffers—imagine Al Gore's spending the entire election campaign explaining why he didn't foresee the crisis."

One of the thousands of Web sites on the Internet devoted to the Year 2000 crisis recorded this anonymous quote: "There are two kinds of people, . . . those who aren't working on it and aren't worried, and those who are working on it and are terrified." Year 2000 computer author Edward Yourdon calls this crisis "Time Bomb 2000" while others refer to this as the "Year 2000 Doomsday Virus."

Some financial experts, including Alan Greenspan, head of the U.S. Federal Reserve Bank, warn that American banks may have to refuse to accept computer data from banks outside the United States if the foreign banks do not correct their computer programs in time.

The problems we face with correcting the Y2K problems are a lack of time, a lack of trained programmers, and a staggering cost, estimated at up to $1 trillion globally to fix the computers. Because of the delay in responding to the clear danger signals, we have simply run out of time to fix all of the critically needed systems before December 31, 1999. There is a desperate shortage of all three elements required to fix the Year 2000 crisis on schedule. One of the worst problems is that we simply do not have the necessary trained computer programmers who know how to check, fix, and test these old computer-programming languages. Industry consultants estimate that we need approximately 300,000 additional programmers, but they do not exist. Just the sheer scope of the challenge of checking, correcting, and testing millions of lines of complex codes is mind-boggling. Some banks, government agencies, and corporations have up to 100 million lines of computer code that must be laboriously corrected. Consultants to the industry warn that we are rapidly running out of time.

Three major areas of computer technology are vulnerable to the Y2K problem: mainframe computers, desktop or personal computers (PCs), and embedded microchips.

Mainframe Computers

The first area of vulnerability is the huge, and often old, mainframe computers and their software programs that are used by countless government agencies (e.g., IRS, Social Security Administration, etc.) to calculate taxes, benefits, and issue tens of millions of checks every month. These giant mainframe computers hold staggering amounts of data that affect every one of us. In addition, many large corporations (including banks, insurance companies, and automobile manufacturers) use these mainframe computers to run their businesses. In most cases, these agencies and corporations could not run for a day without the use of their computer systems. The volume of daily transactions makes it impossible to go back to handling data manually.

These computer systems use millions of lines of computer instructions, or computer code, to tell the computers what to do. A large bank or agency (like the Social Security Administration) might have as many as 100 million lines of computer code that must be meticulously examined to locate the two-digit date field, corrected to read four digits, and then tested over a period of months to make sure the corrected software works properly and is error-free.

The primary problems with fixing mainframe computers and correcting their date fields to operate correctly after 2000 are that we have almost run out of time and there are not enough trained computer programmers who know how to fix the problem. Even before the Year 2000 problem surfaced, industry experts warned that America was unable to find the 200,000 computer programmers that were needed to work with these computers. The overwhelming demand for 300,000 additional trained, competent programmers to work on the Y2K problem means that many government agencies and corporations may be unable to fix all of their computer programs in time because they have either procrastinated or have failed to take seriously the risk to their organization posed by the problem.

Desktop or Personal Computers

The second area of concern is the danger from errors and crashes in the hundreds of millions of personal computers (PCs) that are found in every organization and in millions of homes in every nation. There are three basic vulnerabilities to your PC.

1) Your computer has a clock and a Basic Input-Output System (BIOS) microchip that calculates time. Unfortunately, as I will document later, a study reveals that the majority of PCs sold before January 1997 have BIOS chips that may miscalculate January 1, 2000 as January 1, 1900. This could produce system errors or may even crash your computer and destroy your data.

2) In addition, your computer's operating-system software (often preinstalled on your computer's hard drive) may also misread the year 2000.

3) Finally, many commercial software packages (including spreadsheets and financial planning software) will not operate correctly unless they are updated.

The good news is that each of these problems is solvable. The bad news is that most computer manufacturers and software providers expect you to pay for the installation of the new Y2K-compliant BIOS chip and the upgraded software. Already threats of class-action lawsuits are beginning to surface from disgruntled purchasers who rightly feel somewhat abused when they realize that the expensive computer and software they purchased in late 1996 will not function correctly three years later. However, if you act now you can fix your computer's problem by replacing the BIOS chip today, rather than wait until the fall of 1999 when you might find yourself at the end of an extremely long lineup outside your local computer store or computer repair depot. In a later chapter, I will explain how you can fix your PC before it crashes in the year 2000. Also, there is good news for those who have purchased an Apple Macintosh computer. This computer's hardware and operating system can handle the year 2000 without errors.

Embedded Microchips

The third area of concern is the greatest challenge of all. One of the most powerful and ingenious inventions of our post–World War II society is the development of integrated circuits, which are now called microchips. These marvels of modern technology condense the computing power of all of the world's computers in 1965 into a single powerful microchip the size of a dime, composed primarily of silicon (sand). These brilliantly designed miniature computers contain millions of tiny transistors and hundreds of thousands of miniature circuits of carefully etched, almost invisible, microscopic wires composed of aluminum, copper, or gold.

The essence of our modern world is that virtually everything is defined by numbers that constantly change (e.g., bank accounts, the stock market index, the targeting data for our nuclear missiles, etc.). One computer consultant succinctly warned of the dangers the Y2K problems pose to a world dependent on the embedded microchip: "The embedded chip problem is huge—potentially affecting our most critical industrial, medical, and military control systems. These systems keep nuclear cores stable; the oil, gas, water, and electricity flowing; they keep our airliners, missiles, and satellites in the air and on course; they keep intensive care units operating; and our high tech military armed and mobile."[2]

In 1995, approximately 3.5 billion microchips were manufactured worldwide. By 1996, the number doubled to 7 billion. In 1997, nearly 10 billion of these chips were manufactured. Therefore, it is probable that approximately 20 billion microchips exist throughout the world today, and each year we add another 10 billion microchips more powerful than the chips made the year before. The most recent generation of microchips can complete millions of calculations per second.

A recent report revealed that the computing power of these miniature integrated circuits has increased by a factor of ten thousand in the years since their invention in the early 1970s. While these tiny chips far surpass the computing power of huge railway-car-sized mainframe computers of the 1960s, their power is available at extremely low costs, due to the economies of mass manufacturing and robots. For example, microchips that provide the music you hear when you open a Christmas card cost as little as fifteen cents, while the chips that provide the computing power in state-of-the-art Macintosh or Pentium computers can cost several hundred dollars.

Microchips monitor countless sensors in security systems, heating and air conditioning equipment, VCRs, microwaves, radios, TVs, pacemakers, and cellular phones. They also control numerous delicate functions in your new car (e.g., monitoring the fuel-air mixture several times a second). Microchips are hidden inside communications and spy satellites in space and in the computer-controlled drill head buried a mile deep in the ocean floor of the North Sea oil fields.

The ability of microchips to perform without error for many years has contributed to their universal introduction into a wide range of household and business products and factory machinery. Embedded microchips have their program "burned in" or hard-wired, and cannot be changed in most cases. Computer experts suggest that as many as 5 to 10 percent of the microchips now in use may miscalculate the year 2000, with the result being that errors could be generated or equipment could simply shut down for maintenance because the chip miscalculates that one hundred years have elapsed since the last maintenance inspection.

Will the failure of these microchips interfere with the daily lives of the average citizen? You should judge this for yourself in light of the following items, commonly found in homes, that contain embedded microchips that could be subject to the Y2K bug. The average North American home contains between fifty and one hundred embedded microchips that monitor and control heat, air conditioning, security systems, lighting, cooking, and refrigeration. During the first few months of the year 2000, will the failure of any of the following pieces of equipment have a negative impact on your family's life?

- Automobile
- Home security system
- Global Positioning System in a Range Rover
- A stereo CD component system and its remote control
- Television
- VCR and its remote control
- WebTV with remote control keyboard
- Digital satellite system and its remote control
- Dishwasher
- Refrigerator
- Time-controlled stove
- Kitchen mixer
- Kitchen toaster
- Kitchen juicer
- Bread maker

- Blender
- Coffee maker
- Microwave oven
- Washer and dryer
- Basement freezer
- Electronic bathroom scale
- Digital thermometer
- Digital controls on exercise equipment
- Child's robot toy
- Child's voice-activated toy
- Child's computer game console
- Personal and laptop computers
- Color computer printer
- Cordless telephone
- Telephone answering device
- Personal pager
- Portable tape recorder
- Fax machine
- Personal copying machine
- Digital signal transfer system with remote control
- Portable minidisk recorder
- Personal calculator
- Camcorder
- Digital camera
- Portable radio
- Clock radio
- New digitally controlled dog-silencing collar

The point of this list is to remind you that an extraordinary number of the machines that make our modern life convenient and safe are run by embedded microchips, whether or not we are consciously aware of this. The failure of a significant number of these household computerized machines may cause many changes in your life in the first few months of the next millennium. The amount of equipment in your office or factory that may also be impacted by the failure of embedded microchips is disconcerting. The impact of the failure of these embedded chips within the machinery that runs our factories, airplanes, and government agencies on January 1, 2000 is almost unthinkable. Even worse, it is almost impossible to find and test these billions of microchips to uncover those that contain malfunctioning date fields. All we can do is wait until the next century begins to see which of these billions of chips fail, and then scramble to replace them or replace the equipment, if necessary.

What Kinds of Y2K Problems Might Occur?

What if the government's mainframe computers are not fixed on time? If the government cannot guarantee the successful, error-free collection of tax revenues by the Internal Revenue Service, it may be unable to transfer payments to the tens of millions of citizens who receive monthly welfare and pension checks. It may be unable to pay millions of soldiers and civilian employees that work for governments at the federal, state, and local levels. The government presently mails out approximately 51 million Social Security checks every month. Can you imagine the chaos and desperation if even 1 or 2 percent of these checks are either missed or calculated incorrectly? That would result in up to a million pensioners calling their local Social Security office each month trying to clear up their problems. The system would be quickly overwhelmed.

How long would the "voluntary" system of income tax and Social Security tax payments be supported by an overburdened population that loses confidence in its government's ability to provide a social safety net for the retired, the disabled, and the unemployed? Our entire system of government and our economy depend on a delicate balance of confidence by each participant that the other members of society will fulfill their responsibilities as agreed.

To date, none of the computer systems in the 9,500 banks in the United States are certified as being 100 percent Y2K-compliant (according to the U. S. Federal Reserve as of May 1, 1998). What if your bank cannot open its doors, take deposits, offer loans, clear checks, or allow cash withdrawals after January 1, 2000? How would you live until the banking system sorted itself out? In one case already, customers of a financial lending company were shocked to find themselves incorrectly charged with ninety-six years of interest payments on their accounts; the company's computers could not accurately make interest calculations when they had to deal with the year 2000.

The infrastructure of every community is threatened by the Y2K problem. You may lose vital public services you have taken for granted all your life, such as heat, light, water, sewage, telephone, security systems, police, hospital medical services, and transportation. Unfortunately, the Y2K crisis will begin in the middle of the winter in North America, Europe, and northern Asia. If the nation's electric power grid, which provides the essential electricity for our society, fails for a few days, or longer, this will endanger the elderly, the sick, and anyone who is infirm. Power shortages could trigger brownouts or blackouts like northeastern North America experienced during the ice storms of the winter of 1998. Millions of people lost their electrical power and heat for up to thirty days. Within a week, all supplies of electrical generators in North America were exhausted.

In addition to these problems, many of the most vital security-system computers that monitor our nuclear plants may fail to maintain the security of the plants. On January 1, 2000, nuclear power plant operators may not be able to access the remote shutdown facility or control the high-security areas in their facilities. Controls governing exposure to radiation may fail. Some commentators in the power industry believe that virtually all nuclear power plants may have to be shut down, due to safety and security concerns. Since nuclear power plants generate over 20 percent of our electrical power, this could present enormous problems. In some states in the Northeast, up to 45 percent of their power comes from nuclear plants. The loss of this amount of electrical power would lead to severe power disruptions in the middle of winter.

Health care services could be affected. Your health center's computer may not be able to accurately record the prescriptions prescribed by your doctor or your medical records of past family illnesses. What would you do if your pharmacy's computerized drug-ordering and delivery system failed to work properly after January 1, 2000, and it could not fill your desperately needed prescription for your mother's heart medication? Many year-2000 expiration dates on prescriptions may indicate to noncompliant computer systems that the prescription has already expired, thus preventing a medically necessary prescription from being refilled.

There could also be problems in our criminal justice system.

Police forces and border guards throughout the world may be unable to track the criminal records and fingerprints of known felons and terrorists. Numerous prisons may mistakenly release convicted prisoners or fail to track those criminals on probation or home detention. *The Toronto Star* (Mar. 30, 1998) reported on one case in which a faulty computer program miscalculated court dates, which caused criminals to be inadvertently released.

Another very practical concern is that this computer glitch may cause millions of false fire alarms and burglar-system alarms that could overwhelm the ability of the police and fire departments to resolve genuine problems. For example, a Y2K study by the government of Texas, which was published on its Web site, revealed that up to 25 percent of the computers in their fire trucks failed when tested for the Year 2000 problem. Even worse, these computer microchips disabled the fire trucks' ignition systems because the computer miscalculated that no maintenance had been performed for one hundred years. Another potential problem is that the computer controlling your community's 911 emergency phone system may suddenly malfunction, leaving your city's population at risk, due to the failure of emergency personnel such as police, firemen, or paramedics to respond to your call for help.

Each of these potential problems illustrates the point that the coming computer meltdown in the year 2000 may stretch our society's vital fibers to the breaking point and jeopardize you and your family's well-being.

Developing a Balanced Perspective on the Y2K Crisis

It is important, nevertheless, to develop a proper and balanced perspective on the Y2K crisis. It is not the end of the world as we know it. The sky will not fall. However, unless most major computer systems are fixed in time (the experts say it is impossible to fix everything before the deadline), we will face severe disruptions to our normal way of life for a period of weeks, months, or, in the worst scenario, a year or more. The evidence is very compelling that the magnitude of the Year 2000 computer crisis will prove to be the most expensive and disruptive man-made technological disaster in history. After a year of detailed study of over two dozen books by computer experts and over three thousand pages of material from other books, magazines, and the Internet, I am convinced that this crisis is real and that we need to take action swiftly to protect ourselves.

One way to look at the extent of this crisis is to consider how World War II affected daily life in North America. While no bombs fell on our cities and no enemy soldiers attacked our homes, World War II dramatically affected the lives of almost every citizen. There were severe shortages and rationing of many consumer items, orders to blackout car headlights, the imposition of heavy taxes, and the radical innovation of millions of women entering the workforce to assist wartime production. I do not want to be an alarmist on the Year 2000 crisis, but I would be remiss in my duty as a Christian communicator if I failed to warn my readers of the very real dangers ahead. It would be wonderful if a miraculous technological solution could save us from this impending crisis, but every computer expert I know insists that the problem is far too complex to suppose that a "magic bullet" solution can solve everyone's Y2K problems. Hundreds of millions of computers throughout the world are interconnected by vast computer systems, all using many different programming languages, to produce the wonders of instantaneous communications, global banking, and our high-tech defense systems. No one likes to be the bearer of bad news, but the evidence is overwhelming and mounting daily that this computer crisis is very real, incredibly costly, and astonishingly complex.

At best, we are likely to face the most expensive and difficult man-made crisis in human history. The Year 2000 computer crisis has the potential to negatively impact nearly every family, company, and government on the planet. As I will explain in later chapters, even if a company or government solves its own Y2K problems, it could still face dangerous and costly computer malfunctions if its Y2K-compliant programs are corrupted by other computer systems that have not yet corrected their own Y2K problems.

In *The Millennium Meltdown*, you will find documentation and quotes from reliable government and computer industry experts that will prove that this crisis is real and that it has the capacity to affect your life in serious and unexpected ways. *The Millennium*

Meltdown will also explore the spiritual aspects of preparing yourself and your family for the major changes that the Y2K crisis will bring to your life, your finances, and your career in the near future.

Also, I will examine this crisis from the perspective of Bible prophecy, because my research suggests that this millennium virus may create an international economic crisis that may motivate the governments of the world to declare a state of global emergency. This would provide an unprecedented opportunity for the global elite to argue for the end of national sovereignty and accelerate the move towards global government—a plan they have been working on for the last six decades—by exploiting the fear the Y2K emergency creates within the general population. It is also quite possible that the banking runs and accompanying liquidity crisis that may unfold as one of the consequences of the Y2K problem will also provide a credible rationale for the abolition of paper currency and coins throughout the world.

The transition to a truly cashless society and the introduction of embedded computer chips with your financial records, I.D., and medical records beneath the skin is now technically feasible. It is fascinating to realize that the rise of a one-world government and the introduction of a numerical device beneath the skin of the right hand or forehead that would enable a person to "buy or sell" was actually prophesied by the ancient prophet John in the book of Revelation almost two thousand years ago. It is one of the final signs that Jesus Christ is about to return to establish his millennial kingdom on earth. This will be explored in a later chapter.

Finally, we will carefully examine a range of practical strategies that you and your family can follow that will prepare you to meet the Y2K crisis with confidence. Initially, many readers may feel somewhat overwhelmed when first learning of the dangers to our economy and lifestyle that the Y2K crisis poses. A worthwhile proverb to remember is "To be forewarned is to be forearmed." The book of Proverbs provides a fundamental spiritual principle that we should all take to heart: "A prudent man foreseeth the evil, and hideth himself; but the simple pass on, and are punished" (Proverbs 27:12). This compelling advice applies to this situation, as well as to all other dangers. The Lord considered this proverb so important that it is repeated again in

Proverbs 22:3. As a Christian, I am encouraged by the Bible's exhortation to prepare for dangerous times while also trusting in our Lord to protect us from these dangers. My purpose in writing this book is to alert you, your family, and your friends to the dangers that lie ahead so that you might avoid the worst of the impact of this impending worldwide crisis.

The Millennium Meltdown will suggest some issues that should be carefully considered by those who have a small business or participate in a ministry or church. There is much you can do to protect your organization. Every day brings this danger twenty-four hours closer. There is no time to waste. I strongly urge you to underline and highlight the parts of this book that apply most directly to your own plan to defend yourself, your family, or organization. Carefully study the checklists of possible danger points and actions you can take now to minimize the adverse consequences of the Y2K crisis. The appendix contains useful resources that you may wish to consider as part of your Year 2000 Contingency Plan. It might be helpful to begin a personal Year 2000 file to hold additional information and practical suggestions about the Y2K crisis, as well as the written responses to the letters you send to your bank, insurance company, etc., asking them to confirm to you that their computer systems are Y2K-compliant.

Finally, I urge you to share the information in this book with everyone you care about while there is still time to take action. The more people learn about this approaching crisis, the sooner the management of government agencies and corporations will make the Year 2000 crisis their number-one priority. Remember: Time is of the essence . . . and the countdown to the year 2000 cannot be stopped.

Notes

1. "The Day the World Shut Down." *Newsweek*, June 2, 1997.
2. *Computer Weekly News*, May 11, 1997.

2

The Year 2000 Computer Problem

Reports that warn "we are running out of time" to fix the Year 2000 computer problem are incorrect. Instead, we should announce from the rooftops that we have *already* run out of time. Almost all knowledgeable computer consultants believe that the government and businesses should have assigned high-priority teams to this problem in mid-1997, at the latest, in order to fix all of our essential government and corporate computer systems before the January 1, 2000 deadline. Although it is fairly simple to find the defective data and correct the computer code, the most time-consuming part of the project is laboriously testing the corrected programs over the following months to make certain that they will operate correctly. Many experts suggest that between 60 and 80 percent of the total project time must be spent testing the corrected codes to be certain that they will work without error in the new century. Tragically, the government and business have procrastinated so long that we have run out of time to fix all of the essential computer systems.

Why Did Computer Programmers Make This Fatal Error?
Once people begin to understand the enormity of the Y2K

problem, they naturally wonder what possibly could have caused very intelligent computer programmers to create complex software that contains such a fundamental flaw. I have discussed this question with many programmers over the last year. Originally, programmers programmed computers with only two digits to record the year ("48" instead of "1948") to save space. The cost of computer memory storage in the early years of the computer revolution was staggering in comparison to today. In fact, the original Hollereth punch cards ("do not fold, spindle, or mutilate") held so little memory storage that it was essential to economize. It's hard for us to appreciate today—when laptop computers can be equipped with an eight-gigabyte hard drive (8 billion bytes of memory)—that in the early decades of the computer revolution, a room-sized computer could hold no more than a megabyte of data (one million bytes). Programmers were applauded when they found ways to abbreviate data.

Even into the 1970s and 1980s, when more powerful computers with larger and cheaper memory capacity were manufactured, programmers continued to use only two digits to record year dates because, by then, the format had become standardized. Preprinted computer forms (e.g., invoices) carried the preprinted number 19 followed by a blank space to be filled in with the last two digits of the appropriate year. Incredibly, even in the mid-1990s, many programmers still created software programs that recorded dates with only two digits, even though the new millennium was approaching rapidly.

Most computer industry specialists believed that the rapid advances in computer design and speed meant that the hardware and software they were working on would be obsolete in a few years and be replaced by new computer systems long before the world entered the next millennium. No one expected that these old mainframe computers would work so well and be so expensive and time-consuming to replace that they would be in use decades later.

One of the most knowledgeable and respected consultants on the Year 2000 crisis is Edward Yourdon. He wrote a best-selling book called *Time Bomb 2000* that I strongly recommend to any reader who wants additional research on this topic. In a recent article, "Sayonara Washington," Mr. Yourdon made the following observations:

> Nobody seems willing or able to say it in simple language, so let me be the one: the federal government is not going to finish its Y2000 project. No maybes, no ifs, ands, or buts. No qualifiers, no wishy-washy statements like 'unless more money is spent' or 'unless things improve.' We're not going to avert the problem by appointing a Y2000 Czar or creating a National Y2000 Commission. Let me say it again, in plain English: The United States federal government will not finish its Y2000 project.... How Washington expects to continue functioning after 1/1/2000 is a mystery to me. How American society expects to continue operating in a 'business as usual' fashion, when half of the federal government agencies stop functioning, is a deeper mystery—and one for which we must all begin planning. . . . All of this is so mind-boggling that it falls into the category of 'thinking about the unthinkable.'. . . Realistically, we can no longer talk about what might happen IF Washington fails to fix its Y2000 problems. Realistically, we have to start talking about what will happen WHEN the Y2000 problem brings the government to its knees.[1]

The Danger to Our Electrical Power Grid

Perhaps the greatest problem facing citizens throughout the world is the possible loss of electrical power caused by improper instructions being issued by noncompliant computer systems that operate the country's power grid. However, a recent review of the power utilities has determined that almost all North American electrical power systems are not yet fully Y2K-compliant. To place this risk in perspective, we need to appreciate that virtually every computer system and piece of equipment in modern society is dependent on the safe, continuous supply of electrical power. During the dangerous ice storms that devastated New England and eastern Canada during the early months of 1998, we had a bitter foretaste of the effects a collapse of the power grid has on our daily lives.

The failure of our computer systems to properly process the year 2000 date may produce similar power grid brownouts and blackouts in numerous parts of North America and many other countries as well. The breakdown of the power grid may bring the rest of our complex modern society to a screeching halt. Worse, without a safe supply of power, it may be impossible, in some situations, to bring the electric power generators back on line. How will our computer programmers fix computer systems without electricity? A massive system-wide power failure could easily bring about a nationwide economic, banking, and employment crisis. Millions of people would be unable to receive funds from their banks, or welfare or social security checks from the government. Companies without electric power to run their equipment or the ability to pay their employees or receive payments from customers would be forced to lay off employees.

The consequences of a major power-system failure and the breakdown of our banking system are hard to exaggerate. Without power and the proper functioning of the government's computers, the whole society could collapse to the level of economic activity in 1900. Furthermore, if the government cannot pay their computer consultants, will those consultants continue to fix the government's computers? Many of these computer programmers would certainly leave their positions to obtain other paying positions or retire to the country until the crisis passes. The full ramifications of a failure of the power grid in the first few months of the new millennium will be dealt with in more detail in a later chapter.

Could the Y2K Crisis Affect Our Economy?

A front-page article that appeared in *The New York Times* on April 2, 1997 described the threat that Y2K problems pose to the economy of the United States government:

> Doomsday scenarios have become a staple of the computer industry trade press. Many articles read like works of science fiction, with images of satellites falling from the sky, a global financial crash, nuclear meltdowns, hospital life support systems shutting down, the collapse of the air-traffic system, and a wayward ballistic missile. . . . Without proper attention now, manufacturers could

grind to a halt as their inventory systems break down. Customer orders could go unfilled. The Internal Revenue Service computers could begin spewing out millions of false tax notices. Bank records of loans and mortgages could become fouled up. Stock transactions could fail to clear.[2]

On June 5, 1997, CNN announced that Smith Barney, the famous stock brokerage firm, had experienced an enlightening introduction to the Year 2000 computer crisis. The report stated that "a computer glitch at Smith Barney overnight briefly put $19 million into each of hundreds of thousands of customer accounts, the brokerage said Thursday morning. . . . Smith Barney spokesman Gordon Andrew said customers were not affected in any way. At some point overnight, he said, roughly $19 million appeared in separate entries for each Smith Barney financial management account. The brokerage has 525,000 such accounts."

The computer programmers at Smith Barney tried to correct some of their Year 2000 problems and decided to test their corrected program on the weekend to verify that their new program would work correctly when January 1, 2000, arrived. Apparently, the programming changes were tested off-line successfully. When the programmers tried to complete a live test, however, the result was a complete computer disaster! The programming changes caused $19 million to be accidentally deposited into every one of Smith Barney's clients' accounts. The error amounted to $10 trillion! Over the next few days, the programmers managed to undo the accidental deposits, and by the end of business, three days later, they had completely solved the problem . . . for now.

Other Examples of Recent Y2K Computer Crashes

To provide you with an understanding of the dangers facing our nation and your potential personal risk, consider some recent examples of computer system crashes caused by Y2K problems that have already occurred.

- Recently a number of retail establishments have found that their credit/debit card scanner systems failed to read credit or debit cards that bore expiration dates of January 1, 2000 or beyond. The automated teller machines rejected these credit and debit cards because their computer systems had refused to accept the year 2000 as a valid date.

- A U.S. government agency, using a common five-year budgeting system, found that their computers crashed because the system could not properly process the fifth budget year, the year 2000.

- Various courts throughout the nation have been thrown into scheduling chaos because the computerized case management system that schedules thousands of pending court cases would not accept probation periods of five-year duration. The year 2000 was read as "oo," which was flagged and rejected as an invalid date.

- Many driving licenses that are due to expire in the year 2000 have been rejected as invalid or expired licenses by car rental agencies.

Studies have revealed that no local or state government in America is fully prepared to operate properly after January 1, 2000. Several computer consultants, including the well-respected Edward Yourdon, have warned that at some point in the next seventeen months, many computer programmers may look around, realize that the government and banking systems are not going to fix their computer systems in time, and decide to visit their cottage or their uncle's farm to avoid the worst technological disaster in the history of mankind. When millions of bank customers worldwide decide that they would rather have the cash in their bank accounts in their own hands rather than in the bank (with all of its well-known computer problems), we may witness the collapse of the banking system and one of the worst banking runs in history. Our central bank system of fractional banking reserves depends on bank customers leaving most of their life savings in their bank accounts so that the bank can safely lend out these funds to other customers at a higher interest rate.

Our whole complex society depends on the government collecting vast amounts of taxes from citizens through the Internal Revenue Service (IRS), and then issuing checks to hundreds of millions of social security and welfare recipients. However, following January 1, 2000, millions of citizens may doubt that the U.S.'s IRS or Revenue Canada will be able to accurately trace their cash income. Our tax systems are "voluntary." However, if taxpayers by the millions figure out that their government's computers are breaking down, as a result of their inability to properly handle the year 2000, many may decide to avoid taxation by failing to properly report their correct income and deductions. What will happen to the government's huge entitlement programs—mandated by law—that assist the old, the sick, and the poor by issuing tens of millions of checks generated by government computer systems?

Computer consultants have determined that many of the desktop computers are not ready for the year 2000 (including almost all desktop IBM-compatible computers purchased before 1997 except for the Apple Macintosh computers). These older computers may produce errors in the year 2000. The MS-DOS and Windows 3.1 operating systems may have problems with the Year 2000. It appears that in the year 2000, Y2K-noncompliant desktop computers may reset their computer date to either the year 1980 or 1984. In a later chapter, I will explain how you can fix your PC so that it will function properly in the next millennium.

The Year 2000 Leap Year Problem

To make matters worse, the year 2000 is also a leap year. Millions of computers throughout the world may not correctly calculate dates or schedules after the year 2000 because their programmers failed to realize that the year 2000 is a leap year. There is a simple reason many programmers failed to anticipate that the year 2000 contains a leap day, February 29.

The normal rule is that: *Every fourth year is a leap year.* However, there is an exception to this rule: *Any year divisible by 100 is not a leap year.* This well-known exception caused many computer programmers to conclude that the year 2000 is not a leap year. However, those who came to such a conclusion ignored the third rule for calculating leap years, the exception to the exception: *Any year divisible by 400 is a leap year.* Therefore, the year 2000 is a true leap year.

The failure of many mainframe computer programmers to account for the fact that the year 2000 is a leap year means that all calculations regarding dates after March 1, 2000 will be wrong by one day. If you think this is insignificant, think again. What will happen to the complex scheduling software programs that control flight schedules, military travel, bus and train schedules, duty rosters for police, firemen, etc., and the complex schedules that control security systems. What will happen when building security systems reject February 29 as a valid date and refuse to open vaults, doors, and elevators?

The Fear of Flying in the Year 2000

The complex aviation computer network connects the operations of 550 airports, over 17,000 aviation suppliers, and more than 290 airlines under the direction of the Federal Aviation Agency (FAA). Tom Brown is the head of the Year 2000 Project of the U.S. Air Transport Association, which includes twenty-seven major airlines and shipping companies that are essential to the American economy. When asked about the dangers of flying in the year 2000, Brown replied, "Airplanes aren't going to fall out of the sky. The issue is whether they will take off." Fortunately, once an airplane is in the air, its computers are relatively immune to the calendar date calculations that will afflict many computer programs. My sources in the aviation industry tell me that the use of calendar dates in plane computer systems is very rare. The major Y2K problems are within the computers that control reservations, maintenance, scheduling, purchasing, food service, etc.

As of June 1, 1998, three major airlines have announced that they may not fly on January 1, 2000 until they are assured that safety concerns have been addressed. Recently, the Dutch airline KLM stated in a press release that it might be forced to ground many of its aircraft on January 1, 2000, if it concludes that certain routes are unsafe because of the Y2K bug. KLM public relations officer Hugo Baas declared, "If we have the feeling by the Year 2000 that we don't control the whole chain of transport . . . then we won't fly that route. Regarding safety, there is no risk we are taking. It could result in aircraft being grounded." In an attempt to prevent the widespread grounding of aircraft, KLM has called for an international symposium on the Year 2000 to be held in Amsterdam in July or August 1998. KLM suggests that as many as 160 date-sensitive computer systems involving commercial aircraft must be corrected before January 1, 2000.

On June 9, 1998, Reuters News Wire reported on a meeting in

Montreal of senior aviation officials regarding airline safety in the year 2000. The world's airline industry is spending $1.6 billion to upgrade the computers on its airlines to assure that they will fly normally. Delta Airlines has assigned over four hundred employees to find and correct the Y2K problems in its computers. Airports around the world are spending billions of additional dollars to fix their obsolete air traffic control computers. In addition, airports must examine and upgrade the many other computer systems that run their parking authority, elevators, maintenance equipment, air conditioning, and security, etc.

One aviation business that could be most adversely affected by the Y2K problem is the reservation and travel agencies. The Sabre Group, one of the largest travel reservation companies in the world, is modifying its computer systems to reject noncompliant 2000 dates to avoid the corruption of their computer system. Because Sabre accepts reservations for flights as many as 333 days in advance, the company already realizes that they are extremely vulnerable to the millennium virus. The practice of rejecting data from Y2K-noncompliant computers could result in many companies being effectively shut out of the aviation economy unless they fix their problems in the months leading up to 2000. Those airlines, service companies, car rental agencies, hotels, and aviation parts suppliers who fail to fix their problems on time may face bankruptcy in 2000.

The air traffic control system governed by the FAA is in a desperate race against time to correct its Y2K problems before the January 1, 2000 deadline. The FAA has over 23 million lines of computer code in 250 mainframe computers across the nation. Incredibly, some of these 250 computers from the 1960s are so old that they still use almost unobtainable vacuum tubes. They run on decades-old software programs that cannot be effectively repaired because none of the programmers that created the original computer code are still in the workforce, or, perhaps, even alive. North American air safety is dependent upon these old IBM mainframe computers, which are extremely vulnerable to the Y2K bug. The problem is so great that IBM refuses to repair them or certify that these machines will operate correctly after January 1, 2000. In fact, IBM has demanded that the FAA replace all of its air traffic control computers before the beginning of the Year 2000 to assure the safety of those who fly. Aside from the problems of finding the huge funds needed to replace the entire air traffic control computer system in the next year, it may be almost impossible to purchase, replace, and test any new computer system in the few months that remain until the Year 2000.

The Railroads Are at Risk for Year 2000 Problems

The entire U.S. and Canadian railroad system is vulnerable to Y2K problems because it is 100 percent dependent on computer systems to operate the enormous number of trains and complicated switches that direct the trains. The majority of North America's food, products, and raw resources are transported from one side of the continent to the other on hundreds of thousands of miles of railroad tracks. This vast enterprise is controlled and monitored by complex computer systems that constantly communicate with each other to ensure, for example, that a particular railway car with peaches from Dallas, Texas, arrives at its targeted destination in the New York railway terminal, for ultimate delivery by truck to your favorite grocery store. This complex distribution system is dependent on millions of embedded microchips and huge mainframe computers. Nearly everything connected with our North American railroad system is computerized. Even the switching of tracks is now completed by computer systems. The men who knew how to manually switch trains have retired long ago. It is impossible to rebuild the old manual system.

The failure of these computer systems because of the Year 2000 problem may lead to devastating consequences. The domino effect may trigger the collapse of numerous businesses that utterly depend on the timely delivery of raw materials and finished products. The possible consequences from this particular Y2K breakdown are almost incalculable.

Not long ago in Warren, Michigan, a large and previously successful high-quality grocery store allowed its upper middle-class clientele to pay for their groceries with credit and debit cards. However, the store's computer suddenly began to experience massive crashes and freezes because it could not process debit and credit cards that expired in the year 2000. Over the next few months, the store's computer suffered over one hundred major crashes and shutdowns, causing untold grief to both customers and store employees. Because of these problems, the store suffered a 40 percent loss of business; customers went elsewhere to avoid long delays and embarrassment as the computer rejected their valid cards. Finally, the store brought lawsuits against the various companies that provided its computer and payment systems.

In another case, customers of a major financial company were startled to receive notices that they were behind in their interest payments. They received bills for ninety-six years of compounded interest payments on their outstanding loan balances. In some cases, the notices announced that the customer's overdue interest arrears for the last ninety-six years amounted to more than fifteen times the size of the original loan.

U.S. Federal Reserve Chairman Alan Greenspan testified to the Senate Banking Committee on February 26, 1998, regarding the Y2K problem as it affects the U.S. banking system. Greenspan admitted that the problem had grown so severe that the Federal Reserve was willing and able to loan the individual banks billions of needed dollars to enable them to fix their noncompliant computer systems. However, one of the significant problems is that the Federal Reserve's system itself is noncompliant. It has yet to fix its enormous computer system, which contains more than 90 million lines of sophisticated computer code. The question that arises is this: How will the U.S. Federal Reserve assist its member banks and lend them billions of dollars to assist them in solving their problems if the supervisory bank itself has not solved its own enormous Y2K problems?

As of April 1, 1998, the Information Technology Association of America, which represents some 2,500 senior computer experts, revealed that not one major bank in the United States is ready for the year 2000. In Australia, the Stock Exchange has issued new rules that demand that every listed company on the stock exchange must declare and document its exposure to the Year 2000 problem, or the exchange will suspend trading in their shares. The Philippines Stock Exchange has issued similar rules, effective December 1998. Most of the stock exchanges throughout the world are expected to follow this trend.

On November 3, 1997, Professor Leon Kappelman posted an Internet brief (www.year2000.com) revealing that the majority of embedded chips are located in oil, gas, petrochemical, nuclear, communications and power generating systems; and that from 5 percent to 50 percent of all chips in those systems will fail due to Y2K. He concluded, "Very little real work is happening. Business as usual may be the death of us this time."

Paul French, the Executive Officer of the Data Services Division of the Iowa Department of Transportation, suggested that many cars, trucks, ships, and railroads may break down after January 1, 2000. He claimed that these conclusions were based on meetings behind closed doors with the top executives of the automobile manufacturers. French stated that the hidden microchips which control the heating, air conditioning, lighting, security alarms, elevators, security systems, and manufacturing assemblies in tens of thousands of corporations and agencies may collapse after 2000. The failure of these microchips may result in the collapse of assembly lines and many other businesses.

The Problem within Various U.S. Government Agencies

Congressman Stephen Horn announced on December 15, 1997 that many of the government's own agencies have reported to the Executive Branch that they will be unable to solve the Y2K problem before the January 1, 2000 deadline. He said that the Department of Defense, for example, has concluded that they cannot solve all of the problems in their 348 million lines of computer code before the year 2012! This is frightening when you realize that their military computers control the most advanced weapon systems on this planet. They control the codes that trigger the launching of our most powerful nuclear missiles.

The Y2K Problems in Europe, Asia, and South America

Despite the obvious problems that afflict North America's computer systems, the problems in Asia, South America, and Europe are much worse. The Europeans have not even seriously begun to address the Year 2000 crisis because they have devoted almost all of their computer programming resources to solve the horrendous problem of adjusting their computers to handle the new European currency. The "euro" will be introduced on January 1, 1999, with the introduction of the European Monetary Union within the major nations of the European Union.

According to *Integration Management* (Feb. 16, 1998), many computer experts estimate that the programming modifications required by the European banks, stock exchanges, and trading firms to make the change to the euro will require a greater investment of time and money than the resources needed to handle the Year 2000 problem. Due to the overwhelming effort required to meet the January 1, 1999 European currency deadline, the European nations and their banks are ignoring the need to solve the Y2K problem. However, the combination of these two horrendous computer programming crises and their fast-approaching deadlines makes it very possible that Europe may be totally devastated if major portions of their computer systems fail on January 1, 2000.

Ed Yardeni, the chief economic forecaster for the powerful German investment banking firm Deutsche Morgan Grenfell (New York), was quoted by my friend Donald McAlvany in his insightful analysis of the Y2K crisis and its potential to impact other nations and institutions by spreading from one computer to another in a manner similar to a computer virus. Yardeni warned, "The Y2K virus has infected all the vital organs of our global body. A failure in one system could corrupt other systems. Software system repairs are not as rigorous as most people believe. There is no silver bullet.... The Year 2000 problem is a serious threat to the global economy."[3]

Although Yardeni's past economic forecasts have usually been characterized by optimism, he has publicly warned that he estimates the odds of a global recession beginning in 2000 are as high as 30 to 40 percent. "The main risk is the domino effect where computer and business failure start out as isolated instances and then spread to other sectors.... Computers are critical to transportation, energy, distribution, payroll, just-in-time manufacturing processes, international trade, delivery of oil supplies, aircraft flying patterns and scheduling—everything is affected by this one."[4] His latest estimate is 70 percent.

Testifying as an expert witness before the U.S. Senate Banking, Housing, and Urban Affairs Committee on November 11, 1997, Yardeni made the following comment:

> The year 2000 Problem is a very serious threat to the U.S. economy. Indeed, I believe that it is inevitable that it could

disrupt the entire global economy in several ways. If the disruptions are significant and widespread, then a global recession is possible. . . . I believe that all businesses, both incorporated and unincorporated, should be required by a new law to publicly reveal their current quarterly outlays on fixing Y2K. They should also be required to reveal their best and worst case projections of such outlays.[5]

Yardeni went on to describe the Year 2000 computer crisis as "a systemic risk that will affect all businesses, all vendors, and all customers." The bottom line of Yardeni's warnings to the Senate was that this millennium computer virus is "a risk to the well being of our entire local, national, and global community."[6]

The Basic Government Strategy

The basis approach of governments throughout the world facing the Year 2000 computer crisis is to follow this public relations strategy:

1) Get their public relations people to talk this problem to death.
2) Create impressive committees of VIPs to create the illusion that the problem is being solved expeditiously.
3) Create large numbers of impressive press releases that pretend to show that the government and industry are ahead of the game and will definitely solve the problem before the deadline.

We must understand that this Year 2000 problem is the greatest technological crisis in the history of the world. Untold millions of computer programs are not ready to handle the Year 2000 date correctly. This is, beyond a doubt, the first man-made disaster in the history of mankind that cannot be evaded because of the approaching inflexible Year 2000 deadline. Either we choose to fix the mainframes, the desktop computers, and the embedded microchips on time, or we will be forced to endure a disaster.

Many people wonder why the governments of the United States and other nations have been so slow in reacting to the overwhelming risk to our society that the Year 2000 crisis presents. R. W. Bemer, a brilliant pioneer in the field of computer programming, is often called the "Father of ASCII" (a fundamental computer communication language used by billions of computers throughout the globe). Bemer described the problem as follows: "Governments acted too late when a single assassination started World War I, and again too late when Hitler began World War II. Their main faults were complacency and disbelief in the danger. Now our lives and well being are in danger from our own lack of foresight, for we have allowed the computer to usurp our thought and action processes. We cannot return to our old ways—we have forgotten how, and it's too late."[7]

There Is No Silver Bullet to Solve This Problem

One of the tragic aspects of this crisis is that many corporations and government agencies have procrastinated, and, consequently, lost precious months in the vain hope that someone, somewhere would come up with a brilliant computer program that would miraculously correct the problem and save us from the impending catastrophe. Unfortunately, all of the respected experts in the field agree that the complex nature of the Y2K problem makes it impossible for a universal "silver bullet" solution. Walt Lamphere, a respected commentator on this complex problem, wrote, "The greatest problem we have before us with Y2K is the present wrong decision of the majority of businesses, government, and even the individual, who thinks that 'someone else will fix it.' We will all soon be involved in the worst of financial chaos, such as the world has not known to this day. The impact will be far more catastrophic than any can imagine, and results, virtually unimaginable."

The Media Coverage of the Year 2000 Problem

Despite the fact that the information about the Y2K computer crisis has been known by specialists for many years, the general and business media have studiously ignored the problem until quite recently. In fact, the first major media article that fully explored the Y2K problem was the cover story of *Newsweek* magazine on July 2, 1997. Another eight months passed before the next major article appeared in the cover story on Y2K in *Business Week* magazine on March 2, 1998. Now that several of the major media have begun to address this issue, I predict that there will be a veritable flood of articles beginning in the summer of 1998 and growing in both intensity and fear in the months leading up to the

January 1, 2000 deadline. However, despite the growing number of articles and books, it may be far too late for the major companies and government agencies to shake off their lethargy and solve the problem before their computer programs crash.

One of the most well-respected authorities in the U.S. government concerning the Y2K crisis is Senator Bill Bennett. This senator is an expert on various technology issues that affect both our economy and our national defense. Senator Bennett recently declared that, "The Two-Thousand problem lies at the heart of our economy. Today our economy runs on the energy of information. To cripple the technological flow throughout the world is to bring it to a virtual standstill. To delay our efforts is to be inexcusably reckless."[8]

The solution to the Year 2000 computer crisis for mainframe computers is rather straightforward and simple. Given sufficient time, any competent computer programmer can find the date fields, correct them, and then test for any errors or bugs before reintegrating the corrected software program back into the mainframe computer. If government and corporate managers had only awakened to the true danger of the Y2K problem to Western society when it was first seriously discussed in 1995 or 1996, they would have assigned the necessary programming resources to fix the noncompliant computers while there was ample time to solve the problem without excessive cost or risk. However, even in the later half of 1998, many top leaders of the government and the business world still doubt that the Y2K problem could possibly destroy their careers and, with it, the stability of our economy.

Despite the obvious dangers to the entire world from the impending collapse of the computer systems, there are many governments and corporations that are trying to proclaim that there are no problems and that everything will be just fine at the onset of the next millennium. As one example of this phenomenon, John Cotterell, the director of the Y2K team at Cap Gemini, the largest computer consulting company in Europe, has announced, "I am confident that essential services will work, but every man, woman, and child will be affected."

Notes

1. Yourdon, Edward. "Sayonara Washington."
2. *New York Times,* April 2, 1997.
3. Yardeni, Ed. *The McAlvany Intelligence Advisor,* February 1998.
4. Ibid.
5. Ibid.
6. Ibid.
7. Bemer, R.W. *The McAlvany Intelligence Advisor,* February 1998.
8. Bennett, Bill. *The McAlvany Intelligence Advisor,* February 1998.

3

The Crash Program to Fix the Computers before the Deadline

Tragically the history of the last few centuries reveals that mankind has a far greater ability to endure disaster than it does to avoid it. The tendency to procrastinate and to evade problems until the last minute is almost universal, especially in large organizations such as governments and corporations. Everyone expects someone else to solve the problem. Furthermore, the well-documented history of the information technology business reveals that the average manager of a computer department will move on to another position approximately every eighteen to twenty-four months. This practice has allowed many department heads to avoid dealing with the expensive and time-consuming Y2K problem, knowing that they would be somewhere else when the inevitable Year 2000 deadline arrived. In interviews with computer experts, they told me often they were considering taking a sabbatical during the late fall of 1999 to avoid the chaos that they believe may overwhelm the computer information industry.

The Gartner Group, an internationally respected computer

consulting company, is an advisor to many major Fortune 500 companies about the dangers of the Year 2000 computer crisis. Gartner has announced that they now estimate that the total cost to fix all computers worldwide will exceed $800 billion. Incredibly, even adjusted to today's dollars, this amount exceeds the total cost of all nations for World War II. In other words, the Year 2000 computer crisis will prove to be the most extensive and expensive project that the world has ever faced.

According to a Reuters news report from New York, the Cap Gemini survey of major corporations reveals that 80 percent of the companies surveyed have vastly underestimated the total costs required to make their computers Y2K-compliant. Perhaps the most amazing discovery in this study, however, is that only 12 percent of those companies—many of them Fortune 500 corporations—were willing to admit their level of Year 2000 readiness in their public annual statements issued to their shareholders. However, the ability or inability of these corporations to deal effectively with the Year 2000 challenge is perhaps the most important factor that will determine their ability to survive in the new millennium.

On June 10, 1998, Bonnie Fisher, the manager of the U.S. Department of Transportation's Year 2000 efforts, admitted that the government is heading for a complete disaster because time had run out. Fisher warned, "We have all platforms and a volume of embedded chip technology. The languages used to create some applications are no longer supported. And they run on platforms that are no longer supported. Right now, the government is dealing with 7,850 different systems." Although the government claims that approximately 30 percent of its computer systems are 2000-compliant, Ms. Fisher stated that this assumption was not based on significant testing or meaningful evaluation. Incredibly, Fisher also admitted, "The U.S. government, until recently, was reluctant to fund any Y2K programs. In the case of many agencies Y2K is an unfunded mandate."[1] In other words, the government expected its individual departments to fix their Y2K computer problems using their existing people and budgets. This reveals incomprehensible complaisance and managerial incompetence in the face of a problem of this magnitude.

Testing Computer Systems for Y2K Vulnerability

The consultants and programmers that are most familiar with the magnitude of the millennium virus warn that almost everyone fails to appreciate the amount of time that is necessary to test a computer system after the detection and correction of two-digit date fields. The experts warn that 60 to 80 percent of a Y2K project may have to be expended on testing the various parts of the program, using all possible date variables. Paul Scott, the assistant deputy minister of the province of Ontario's Year 2000 Initiative, is responsible for the government's response to the millennium crisis. On June 5, 1998, Scott informed a group of consultants that the Y2K testing phase for Ontario's Department of Transportation took twice as long as they had initially calculated. He stated that another department's computer conversion took six times as long as initially planned. The current estimate to fix all of the computers for the Canadian government exceeded $12 billion, while they believed the cost to fix Y2K throughout the world would exceed $1 trillion.

Even testing for the Year 2000 bug can be extremely dangerous for a corporation or government agency. The process of searching for Year 2000 errors can actually trigger massive computer failures. Recently, I began receiving reports that fixing Y2K programs in itself can destroy data. When a number of companies and government agencies began to test their date-field corrections in the Y2K-modified computer programs, they found that occasionally they triggered catastrophic errors, system crashes, and even the total loss of entire databases. It turns out that the very act of searching for the date fields in an old mainframe computer program often leads to the destruction of data.

For example, the National Pharmaceutical Association in the United Kingdom recently reported that two major pharmaceutical corporations tested their computer systems for their ability to function correctly after January 1, 2000 and inadvertently wiped out their entire corporate records, producing a complete disaster. Another British government department was testing its computer systems to see if they would continue to operate properly in the year 2000 and was shocked to discover that the introduction of the year 2000 date caused irreparable damage to its files. The government department could not recover its valuable data. As the panic has grown, the four major banks in the United Kingdom have pledged to spend over one billion pounds (over 2 billion U.S. dollars) to correct their Year 2000 problems. The major executive departments of the U.K. have budgeted almost £400 million, while the U.K. health department expects to spend more than £500 million to fix their computers that handle patient records, ambulances, and nurse rotation.

Capers Jones, the Chairman of SPR, Inc., is considered to be one of the most knowledgeable experts in the world on the problem of estimating the cost and time necessary to solve the Y2K crisis. In his authoritative study on the practical difficulties of managing the massive computer programming changes necessary to prepare a company or a government to survive the millennium meltdown, Capers Jones wrote, "The year 2000 problem is unique in human history. There has never been a man-made technical problem that will affect so many businesses, so many government groups, and cause so many problems at a personal level. The Year 2000 problem is unique in that it has at least the potential to effect more computer systems at the same time than any other event except the electromagnetic pulse from a nuclear explosion."[2] In his company's exhaustive report on the Y2K problem, "The Global Economic Impact of the Year 2000 Computer Software Problem," Capers Jones wrote that the devastating impact of the Y2K crisis will be "the most expensive single problem in human history."[3]

Jones is one of the most qualified experts in the world regarding the true costs of software development and repair programs. Jones suggests that the ultimate costs to correct our North American computer systems are far greater than the politicians have admitted and may exceed $250 billion. He states that "The Year 2000 repair costs may exceed $2000 for every working person in the United States, or more than $900 for every citizen of the United States."

In the spring of 1998, Robin Guenier, the well-respected former chief advisor on the Y2K computer crisis for the British government, revealed that his experts calculated that fixing the Y2K problem for the United Kingdom's government computers would exceed $130 billion, and that, in his estimation, the United Kingdom had run out of time to fix all its computers and that "a satisfactory solution was now impossible." Since the Labour Party has taken over the U.K. government, Gwynneth Flower is now the director of Action 2000, which is advising the government on the problem. Flower warned that Y2K, if not fixed by January 1, 2000, is "a problem that could bring down a government."

It is astonishing to realize that, with only a year and a few months to go, only 16 percent of businesses in the United Kingdom have even begun to repair their computer code. Although many inquiries have been made regarding the readiness of the essential utilities to function in the next century, not one major utility in the United Kingdom has publicly confirmed that its water and sewage systems will work properly. In addition, British Telecom, which runs a large portion of the U.K.'s telecommunications industry, has admitted that they cannot guarantee that its customers will be able to make or receive calls in the opening days of the year 2000.

After years of basically ignoring the computer consultants who were like prophets crying in the wilderness about the coming Y2K catastrophe, the world press has finally awakened, at least partially, to the approaching crisis that will impact all our lives. The *Washington Post* ran an article on September 15, 1996 in which the writer declared, "For some institutions, it will soon be too late. We could end up with a real catastrophe that could affect many people's lives around the globe. . . . One industry expert has called the (Y2K) defect 'the most devastating virus ever to infect the world's business and information technology systems.'"

The computer consulting industry has admitted that it lacks the trained computer programmers that are needed to solve this computer crisis. Computer consultants have estimated that up to 300,000 additional programmers are required to solve this crisis in the limited time that remains until January 1, 2000. According to a cover story in *Business Week* magazine on March 2, 1998, the demand for additional computer programmers to fix the nation's computers has resulted in the hiring of 200,000 new programmers over the last twenty-four months. An additional concern is that the limited number of programmers combined with the rapidly approaching January 1, 2000 deadline has already caused a massive inflation of the wages and bonuses that such programmers can earn. Numerous computer companies have begun offering enormous bonuses to their existing employees to encourage them to remain on the job, and not accept alternative job offers from competitors. Reports are circulating about offers of bonuses of up to $100,000 to programmers who are willing to leave their employers and join a new firm.

Triage Computer Salvage Operations

Despite all of the crash emergency programs, some computer experts are finally suggesting that we must analyze our overall systems to determine which of them are absolutely mission critical and must be saved. All other systems, no matter how important, that are not absolutely critical to the survival mission of the corporation or the government agency must be set aside until after we survive the immediate Year 2000 crisis—a dilemma analogous to the medical triage officer who must examine overwhelming numbers of battle casualties to determine which of the injured soldiers can be saved by the limited medical facilities available and which soldiers must be allowed to die because there is a lack of doctors and medicine.

United Kingdom Prime Minister Tony Blair has called for the creation of a "Millennium Virus" army of up to 20,000 new, trained computer programmers who will be prepared by special training programs to assist companies in their efforts to fix their Y2K problems before the approaching deadline arrives. The U.K. government will offer £1,300, or approximately $3,000 to interested people who are willing to be trained to assist the national Year 2000 computer effort. However, a recent study by *The Sunday Times* newspaper concluded that the United Kingdom desperately needed up to 30,000 well-qualified computer programmers to work on this project while America needed over 340,000 programmers. Unfortunately, these programmers do not exist and it is very unlikely that new volunteers can be trained in the few months that remain until the inflexible deadline arrives. The report noted that American companies were so desperate to acquire Y2K professionals in the U.K. that they were offering qualified staff as much as $13,000 per day as well as guaranteed Concord flights home to visit their family every weekend.

The Bank of America has admitted that it is spending over $350 million to fix its Y2K problems, with a huge portion of their budget allocated to paying salaries, bonuses, and stock options for qualified programmers, to induce them to join the bank and to stay until the crisis is passed. Every month the salaries offered to trained COBOL programmers rises dramatically, reflecting the worldwide shortage of qualified programmers who understand the old computer languages such as COBOL, FORTRAN, JOVIAL, etc. unfamiliar to the thousands of graduating computer students. Although America graduated over 26,000 computer science students last year, only a small percentage were trained in those old computer languages used by the mainframe computers that run our largest corporations and government agencies.

Most new computer graduates and their professors are training to work with the exciting new computers and the newer programming languages including Code Warrior and C++. Many graduates have little interest in the older, obsolete computer languages because they see them as a career dead end. Over five hundred computer languages have been used over the last forty years. Many of these languages are obsolete and practically unknown by the young computer programmers who are working today. However, the worldwide shortage of trained programmers who can examine hundreds of millions of lines of old computer code will produce a devastating result over the coming months.

Peter de Jager, one of the world's foremost consultants on the Y2K problem, states that the major North American corporations might fix the worst of their computer problems if they choose to treat this problem as a World War II Manhattan Project. He notes that, "The only question is are we smart enough to do it sooner rather than later."[4]

Notes

1. Manktelow, Nicole. "US Heads for a Y2K Calamity." *The Australian* Internet, June 10, 1998.

2. Jones, Capers. *The Year 2000 Software Problem.*

3. Jones. "The Global Economic Impact of the Year 2000 Computer Software Problem." SPR, Inc., 1996.

4. Zuckerman, M. J. *USA Today.* June 10, 1998.

4

How the Y2K Crisis Will Affect Your Health, Family, and Home

The Medicare Health Care Catastrophe

In 1997, over 38 million American citizens received Medicare checks to pay for needed medical and health services. A May 16, 1997 report by the General Accounting Office (GAO) entitled "Medicare Transaction System," concluded that, on average, in the year 2000 there will be over a billion claims amounting to over $288 billion. The approaching disaster may cause the collapse of the Medicare system. According to the GAO report, the existing Medicare system (upon which millions of citizens depend) may simply not survive the transition to the new millennium. The reason is that the managers who administer this federal health system have made two disastrous decisions that will adversely affect the lives of many Americans. It turns out that the millions of medical claims are not actually processed by Medicare itself, but by seventy private corporations. The first problem is that Medicare never enacted a plan to ensure that the Year 2000 virus was eliminated from the computers of these seventy corporations that administer the claims. Therefore, the Medicare system is almost certain to collapse, following December 31, 1999.

The second problem is that Medicare announced that it will not renew the contracts of the seventy administrating corporations in the year 2000 because it has decided to set up a new centralized computer system to administer the claims within the agency. Medicare sent letters to each of the seventy fired agencies asking them to spend millions of their own dollars to convert their systems and data to make them Y2K-compliant before handing everything back over to the government's agency on December 31, 1999. The GAO report concluded, with admirable under-statement, that these fired "contractors may not have a particularly high incentive to properly make these conversions." The GAO report concluded that the Health Care Financing Administration (HCFA), which oversees Medicare operations, will fail in 2000 because of its failure to create any contingency plans. "HCFA officials are relying on the contractors to identify and complete the necessary work in time to avoid problems." However, the report noted that the "contractors not only have not developed contingency plans, they have said that they do not intend to do so because they believe that this is HCFA's responsibility." The GAO experts believe that the chances of these seventy fired corporations completing this Year 2000 conversion are between slim and none.

Another nearly insurmountable problem is the difficulty of Medicare's computer consultants to successfully develop a new, all-encompassing in-house computer system in time for the handover, as we reach the new century. The history of the total failure of the Internal Revenue Service to modernize and centralize its own computer systems during the last eleven years, despite spending over $4 billion, does not suggest that Medicare is likely to succeed either. Tragically, for millions of citizens who depend upon this government system to pay their medical bills, it is almost certain that Medicare, as we know it, will face disaster when their computers crash. The General Accounting Office report concluded, "Unless timely, effective systems changes are implemented as the year 2000 approaches, HCFA may be unable to process claims accurately and within required time frames. The potential risks associated with not being ready for 2000 are serious, since virtually all Medicare transactions depend, to some degree, on dates to determine benefits eligibility—dates of birth, medical procedure, other insurance coverage, and so forth."

Recently, reports from Australia suggest that the refusal of insurance companies to cover doctors and hospitals from the risks associated with Y2K problems will have a devastating impact on the availability and costs of medical services. Maurice Newman, the head of the Australian Stock Exchange, warned those who work in the medical field that the insurance companies that provide their professional indemnity policies will almost certainly exclude any Y2K-related insurance claims on the legal grounds that the problem was one that easily could have been foreseen and corrected. Newman, who is also the chairman of the Year 2000 Steering Committee, told the medical profession that they could not depend on their medical malpractice insurance policies to protect them if patients sued due to problems caused by their computers' malfunctioning. He warned that the millennium virus is the greatest threat in history to the Australian public's health.

Newman stated that the computer's inability to handle dates in the new century was a "highly contagious, all pervasive disease which unless controlled will assume epidemic proportions." He warned the medical profession that potentially the entire health industry is at risk from massive lawsuits from health problems, resulting from the Year 2000 problem, which will not be covered by the insurance industry. If his prediction proves correct, many health practitioners and the pharmaceutical industry may decide that it is an intolerable risk to continue to provide medical services. If the doctors' insurance companies refuse to cover the Y2K risk, and the hospital's own insurance companies try to avoid covering this insurance risk, a great number of health care professionals may refuse to expose their families and their personal assets to the risk of lawsuits and may limit the medical services they are willing to provide. The legal risks to the directors of hospitals are overwhelming, unless their insurance policies will protect them from Y2K risks. It may be necessary for governments to enact laws that will provide blanket protection to health care professionals from Y2K lawsuits in order to ensure the continued availability of medical services in the next millennium.

The Y2K Risk to Medical Equipment

During the last fifty years, medical science has made significant advances, including the invention of marvelous medical devices that monitor the body's systems, facilitate surgery, and contribute in countless ways to our improved health and life span. However, many of these essential medical devices may fail when we reach the next century because they include miniature embedded microchips. The average hospital utilizes up to 30 separate mission-critical computer systems and more than 14,000 medical devices that depend on computers or embedded microchips. In addition, many hospitals use up to 5,000 personal computers, as well as mainframe computers and embedded chips that control the hospital infrastructure, including monitoring medical gases, air conditioning, heat, and elevators.

On April 27, 1998, a report on the dangers to our health care medical equipment from the millennium virus appeared in the *Pittsburgh Business Times.* John Grimm, head of information services for the Hospital Council of Western Pennsylvania, warned about the risks within his hospital group: "There are potentially 10,000 to 15,000 medical devices that could be affected." The article also reported, "Magnetic resonance imaging machines, CAT scan equipment or high-tech patient monitoring devices all have potential problems due to the coming of the year 2000. These devices contain what are known as 'embedded chips'—computer chips that control certain aspects of the machine's operation, and which may be subject to the Y2K bug. The problem is you don't know which ones will be affected and which ones won't.... The consequences of having noncompliant chips could range from business simply being conducted as usual to a total shutdown."[1] The good news is that the three major manufacturers of pacemakers and defibrillators, which monitor over half a million hearts in North America, have confirmed that their devices will continue to operate properly because their chips do not depend on calendar calculations.

The same Y2K health concerns that threaten the United States also impact the National Health Services (NHS) in the United Kingdom. They now estimate that they will be forced to spend up to $1 billion on converting their computers to allow the health ministry to function in the new century. An Internet news release by the BBC on May 15, 1998 reported that "The [U.K.] Department of Health has described the millennium bug as an unprecedented threat to the NHS." In the same article David Davis, the chairman of the Commons Public Accounts committee, responded to the NHS Y2K report by saying, "Much of the equipment used in diagnosis and treatment, for example, intravenous infusion pumps used commonly in the NHS, contain embedded microprocessors. Failures of such vital pieces of equipment could have even more serious consequences for individuals than failure of major computer systems." As one example, St. Bartholomew's Hospital in London now estimates that if only 10 percent of the National Health Services computer system succumbs to Y2K problems, that failure would likely cause the premature deaths of as many as 1,500 patients.

The Year 2000 Crisis Threatens Your Vital Medications

There are millions of people that need oral medications or daily injections to live a normal life. Despite the fact that spokesmen for the pharmaceutical industry assure us that there is no Y2K problem in their industry, the fact that computers are involved in every area of the pharmaceutical industry suggests that their computers will suffer from significant breakdowns and errors in the early months of the next century. For example, millions of North Americans with diabetes require daily doses of insulin. However, 70 percent of the entire world's supply of insulin is manufactured in one highly computerized manufacturing plant in the Netherlands. Additionally, the continuous supply of any medication depends upon the uninterrupted delivery of medications from pharmaceutical companies that are susceptible to Y2K computer problems. Each manufacturing plant is at the disposal of its chemical suppliers, banks, marketing distributors, as well as its utilities, including the phone company and the utilities supplying water and sewage.

The Risk of Y2K Is Not Confined to January 1, 2000

One of the dangers of the Y2K crisis that is rarely discussed is the fact there are several dates related to the year 2000 that will expose our complex international computer networks to the risk of systemic failure. The computer specialists who are fighting to control the damage call these dates "spike dates" or "key dates." Without going into all of the intricate reasons, I can assure you that a number of critical computer programs will encounter severe problems long before January 1, 2000 because of the decisions made by computer programmers decades ago. One problem is that some programmers created program instructions in which the appearance of the year "99" in the year-date field was made to signify an instruction to the computer to shut down and erase all data. Although it seems senseless today, these programmers never thought that governments and corporations would still use these computers in the final years of this century. Inadvertently, these programmers have created a potential nightmare unless this outdated code is corrected in time.

The Y2K computer experts at Coopers and Lybrand accountants warn that there are eight separate dates that will occur in the coming years that may possibly trigger computer problems in systems that are not Y2K-compliant.

- The final week of December 1999
- The first week of January 2000
- January 31, 2000
- February 29, 2000
- The fiscal year end of the year 2000
- The final week of the year 2000
- The first week of the year 2001

While each of these dates poses less risk than January 1, 2000, the computer experts who study this problem agree that many computer systems will begin showing various unusual symptoms when their computers fail to calculate accurately on these approaching dates.

Will the Year 2000 Adversely Affect My Personal Computer?

The vast majority of the Internet sites and articles in technology magazines dealing with the Y2K problem have focused almost exclusively on the impending dangers to the thousands of aging mainframe computers used by government and corporations in every nation. However, the problem of mainframe computers is only one-third of the overall crisis the world is facing on January 1, 2000. Another third of the problem is hundreds of millions of personal computers (PCs) that are found in government agencies, banks, insurance companies, corporations, and homes throughout the world.

The brilliant advances in computer technology in the last few decades have allowed the average businessman or home owner to purchase a personal computer for only a few thousand dollars that packs more computing power than the railway-car-sized computers that existed in laboratories in the 1950s. Unfortunately, the same computer software programming habits that produced the Y2K problem in the mainframe computers affect personal computers as well. Software programmers have been privately talking and joking about this problem for years. However, the evidence is overwhelming that, as late as 1996, they were still designing most computer hardware and software using only two digits to represent the year. These systems will fail disastrously. One study found that up to 93 percent of personal computers manufactured before 1996 will not handle the year 2000 properly.

When the personal computer revolution began in approximately 1984, the hardware designers placed an embedded microchip on the circuit board that keeps accurate time and relays that precise time to any program that needs it for calculations. This quartz crystal, like the one in your watch, keeps incredibly accurate time and stores this time data on an embedded chip known as the Real Time Clock (RTC). Unfortunately, the programmers designed the Real Time Clock to calculate the time and the year with the year designated by two digits. The Basic Input-Output System (BIOS) microchip works with the Real Time Clock to tell the computer and its software the correct time and year. These embedded chips exist in every PC. We are now learning that the vast majority of BIOS chips made before 1996 will fail to work correctly in the next century. Fortunately, it is possible to fix this problem yourself if you are handy with your computer's hardware, or, for the rest of us, if you take your computer to the local computer repair store and have them install a new Y2K-compliant BIOS replacement chip. This repair is quite simple and fast, and I strongly suggest that you call your computer repairman now, before a hundred million other PC owners begin a rush to fix their computer.

Leon Kappelman, the editor of the *Year 2000 Journal*, warns that the media have almost ignored the PC problem because the mainframe computer problem is enormous. Karl Fielder is a respected U.K. computer consultant who gave a speech on the PC problem at the SPG Year 2000 Conference. As reported by the *Chicago Tribune* in an article called "Look Out PC, Here Comes Your Y2K Crisis," Fielder's speech was aptly entitled, "If You Can Sleep Properly at Night, You Don't Understand the Significance of the PC Problem." Fielder warned, "The PC problem is horrendous. We conducted the largest-ever independent testing of PC programs and hardware. We have tested the Basic Input-Output System, or BIOS, on over 500 types of PCs, and of those machines made before 1997, 93% failed the BIOS test. This is very real and will have a far-reaching effect."[2]

Fielder revealed the following results of their study: "Out of 4,000 tested PC programs only 28% claimed to be Y2K-compliant; 44% didn't know that 2000 is a leap year; 3.5% only work in the 20th century; and 11.5% store dates different from the user input. There is, however, encouraging news. Of the computers that have come out in 1997, we're finding that only 47% fail."[3] Incredibly, despite the publicity within the industry, his study shows that half of the PC manufacturers were still endangering their customers' businesses, etc., by installing Y2K-noncompliant BIOS chips in 1997, as the crisis looms just in front of us. Fielder made the following comment regarding our PCs' vulnerability to this crisis: "I think that this problem is going to be far worse than anyone expects."

Dr. Gary North, a well-known and respected researcher, has written extensively on the Internet about the dangers to your PC due to Year 2000 noncompliance. I highly recommend that you bookmark his Web site: Gary North's Y2K Links and Forums (http://www.garynorth.com/y2k/). Dr. North makes the following cogent remark: "There are about 250 million PCs out there. If they run on DOS, they aren't 2000-compliant. If they run on Windows 3x, they aren't 2000-compliant. If they have not had their BIOS chips replaced, they aren't compliant. If they are running any piece of software that is not compliant, they aren't compliant. Think of a spreadsheet that isn't compliant, but which still keeps running . . . wrong."

Dr. North also points out the incredible problems that the IRS faces because of a law that Congress recently passed regarding income tax filing: "It is law in the United States that all Internal Revenue Service quarterly payments be submitted by computer in the year 2000. What if these PC computers are not compliant? Most of them won't be. . . . What happens to world productivity when 230 million out of 250 million PCs either shut down or start scrambling their programs? What happens to networks? What happens to insurance companies and banks that rely on PCs to input data?"

Now for some good news! If you have an Apple Macintosh computer, you have made an inspired choice. They are the only manufacturers of personal computers to date that are known to be fully Y2K-compliant. While your Macintosh computer and its Mac operation system are year 2000-compliant, you still need to make certain that your favorite software does not have hidden year 2000 problems. If one of your favorite software applications was originally created for Windows systems and ported over to work on the Macintosh computer, you might find limited problems. It is still advisable to check with the software manufacturer or their Internet Web site to be certain the software application is compliant. Fortunately, most Macintosh owners will be able to use their computers in the next millennium without problems. More good news is that all major software manufacturers have Web sites on the Internet that will allow you to freely download their Year 2000 software fix to make their software application work properly in the next century.

However, if you belong to the vast majority of personal computer owners, you decided to purchase a computer from IBM or from one of a multitude of IBM clone manufacturers that exist. Unfortunately, most of these machines, if purchased before 1997, will display a number of significant Year 2000 errors when we reach January 1, 2000. The problems you face are derived from two different aspects of desktop computing. First, the PC computers themselves contain a Basic Input-Output System (BIOS) component that maintains an accurate record of the current date, along with many other basic functions. However, like many mainframe computers, a large number of personal computers manufactured in the last fifteen years have a BIOS chip that calculates years using only two digits. When January 1, 2000, arrives, many of the personal computers that are found in millions of homes and in tens of millions of businesses will find that they are unable to correctly make the transition to the year 2000. Consequently, these PCs will make incorrect calculations in numerous programs that will make nearly all of their results unreliable.

Greenwich Mean Time, a computer consulting company in England, has analyzed the danger of the Y2K problem to the hundreds of millions of personal computers that sit on the desktops of homes, businesses, and governments throughout the world. After examining the personal computer BIOS systems of more than 500 different computer configurations, they issued a report that concluded that despite the growing awareness of the danger posed by the approaching Year 2000 deadline to the operations of both computer hardware and software, 97 percent of the personal computers manufactured before 1997 are not ready to handle the year 2000. Incredibly, only 53 percent of the personal computers manufactured in 1997 are ready to handle data properly after January 1, 2000.

Billions of Hidden Embedded Chips Will Fail

Billions of embedded computer chips are hidden in the equipment and machinery that make our lives safe, efficient, and comfortable. Many experts believe that as many as 10 percent of these chips may not successfully operate after the January 1, 2000 deadline. These chips are hard wired with their computer program "burned in" to the chips' circuitry. In almost all cases, they cannot be reprogrammed. If they fail to operate correctly after the year 2000, the only option is to replace the failed chip. However, in many cases these tiny computer chips are hidden deep within machinery and are often almost inaccessible. Other chips are inaccessible because they are located in space satellites or deep within cables or equipment beneath the sea. It is virtually impossible to test such chips before they fail. Therefore, we will not know for certain the extent of this problem until these chips start failing all over the world on January 1, 2000.

These hidden computer chips have a variety of uses. They make sure that the oil flows properly at the underwater well head of offshore oil rigs thousands of feet below the surface in the North Sea. They stabilize nuclear cores in dangerous atomic energy plants. They monitor the flow of sewage, water supplies, and electricity. Most dangerous of all are the millions of embedded chips that control the missiles and weapons. How many embedded chips are out there? Manufacturers such as Intel and Motorola produced and shipped 3.5 billion microchips in 1995, 7 billion chips in 1996, and almost 10 billion computer chips in 1997.

Complicating the problem of finding and replacing microchips is the fact that a number of chip manufacturers are either out of business, have merged with other businesses, or are no longer making the same type of chip.

Most likely these embedded chips will operate perfectly until January 1, 2000, when as many as 10 percent of these vital microchips will simultaneously fail without warning, plunging many critical infrastructure systems into chaos. Other embedded chips that are not in continuous use may fail only when they are switched on for the first time in the year 2000. An additional problem with embedded microchips is that most of them were designed to read only positive integers or dates. When they first encounter the unexpected date field "oo" representing the year 2000, these chips may fail because the number "oo" is not positive and will not be recognized as a proper positive integer. Many chips will fail because they will interpret the "oo" to mean "null," or "zero," and will shut down in confusion.

Notes

1. *Pittsburgh Business Times,* April 27, 1998.

2. "Look Out PC, Here Comes Your Y2K Crisis." *Chicago Tribune,* September 30, 1997.

3. Ibid.

5

Y2K Electrical Power and Utility Failures

The Dangers to the National Electrical Power Grid

Almost everything in modern society depends upon the safe, reliable, and continued supply of electrical power. We have come to depend upon and expect the presence of safe, reliable electrical power as much as we have a natural expectation that there will be air to breathe tomorrow. However, one of the greatest dangers facing our society in the year 2000 is that this previously reliable electrical power generation may be jeopardized by the Y2K problem. Nearly every component of our increasingly complex electronic power grid depends on sophisticated computer programs and programmable computer controllers that direct the whole process of delivering reliable electricity to the nation's homes and factories. Studies indicate that not one of the U.S. electrical power systems was Y2K-compliant as of July 1, 1998.

Major electrical utilities warned the United States Senate during hearings on June 12, 1998 that Y2K may cause lights to go out across America following New Year's Eve, 1999. The officials of the utilities admitted that the millennium bug will begin to affect millions of embedded microchips, mainframe computers, and desktop computers throughout the vast infrastructure of the North American electrical power grid that may cause devastating power losses. Incredibly only twenty percent of the major utilities examined by the Senate's Special Committee on the Year 2000 had even completed their initial Y2K assessment of their vital mission critical systems. It is astonishing to discover that not one major utility in America has even developed contingency plans to cope with the massive computer failures they now know will impact their essential industry. Senator Christopher Dodd warned, "We're no longer at the point of asking whether or not there will be any power disruptions, but we are now forced to ask how severe the disruptions are going to be."

Furthermore, the U.S. Nuclear Regulatory authorities may need to shut down all nuclear power plants that are not Y2K-compliant. Rick Cowles, a Y2K professional advisor to the U.S. electrical power industry, has warned in February 1998 that, "Not one electric company has started a serious remediation effort on its embedded controls. Not one. Yes, there's been some testing going on, and a few pilot projects here and there, but for the most part it is still business as usual, as if there were ninety-seven months to go, not ninety-seven weeks."[1] In addition to their own internal Y2K computer problems, our power grid is vulnerable to the loss of coal fuel if the train system is disabled by its own Year 2000 computer problems. If power plants fail to receive coal supplies for only thirty days, they will begin shutting down across North America.

In the United States, the federal government's senior regulator (in charge of energy utilities) has warned that a number of major American electrical power and fuel supply corporations have not determined the level of their exposure to the millennium virus. Recently, Kathleen Hirning, the chief information officer of the Federal Energy Regulatory Commission (FERC), warned the U.S. House of Representative's subcommittee on science that without extensive Year 2000 testing it is absolutely impossible to accurately determine the amount of disruption from noncompliant systems and the ripple effect their failure may cause throughout the nation's power grid. The latest reports from the electricity and gas industries in the U.K. indicate that they are in precisely the same situation. They are flying blind into a most dangerous storm. Not only are U.K. regulators admitting that they are in the dark about their nation's power utilities' readiness for the year 2000, they admit that they lack the legal regulatory powers under the 1989 Electricity Act to demand that the power companies fix the Y2K problem on time. Unfortunately, the news from Europe, Asia, and South America is even worse. Their utilities are essentially unaware of the approaching danger.

The most significant concern is that the power grid is utterly dependent on extremely sensitive computer monitoring equipment to effectively transfer surplus electricity from one area of the nation to another area. The electrical power grid is very complex and must be very carefully monitored to avoid power surges and complete systems failure. Every transfer of electricity is monitored and recorded. All of this complicated routing of electrical transmission depends on instantaneous computer calculations that could fail if the power grid's computer systems succumb to the Year 2000 bug. Most worrisome of all, the communications between the computers and the human supervisors are utterly dependent upon reliable telecommunications. If the telephone system fails, it is almost certain that our power grid will fail simultaneously, turning the lights out across North America.

A March 1998 article in *Business Week* said the following:

> In particular, electric utilities are only now becoming aware that programmable controllers, which have replaced mechanical relays in virtually all electricity-generating plants and control rooms, may behave badly or even freeze up when 2000 arrives. Many utilities are just getting a handle on the problem. "It's probably six months too soon for anyone to try to guess the complete extent of the problem," says Charlie Siebenthal, manager of the Year 2000 program at the Electric Power Research Institute, the industry group that serves as an information clearinghouse. "We don't know if electricity flow will be affected," he said.[2]

Nuclear Power Plants Vulnerability to Y2K

The same article in *Business Week* also addressed the issue of nuclear power plants:

> Nuclear power plants, of course, pose an especially worrisome problem. While their basic safety systems should continue to work, other important systems could malfunction because of the 2000 bug. In one year 2000 test, notes Jared S. Wermeil, who is leading the millennium bug effort at the Nuclear Regulatory Commission, the security computer at a nuclear power plant failed by opening vital areas that are normally locked. For that reason, the NRC is in the process of issuing a letter requesting confirmation from utilities that their plants will operate safely come January 1, 2000. Given the complexity and the need to test, "it wouldn't surprise me if certain plants find that they are not Year 2000-ready and have to shut down," says Wermeil.[3]

The American electrical power industry is now bracing itself for the most massive engineering challenge in the history of the United States. The latest reports suggest that as of June 1, 1998 perhaps a third of America's electrical utilities were not even working on the Y2K problem seriously (according to an industry survey by the well-respected Gartner Group). Of the more than 9,000 electrical power plants across the nation, not one was Year 2000-compliant as of the spring of 1998. The probability is that between 25 to 30 percent of the power utilities will experience at least some computer problems in the early months of the Year 2000 that will lead to some service interruptions. Some commentators worry that problems with embedded microchips may cause system-wide failure for short periods as the national power grid attempts to deal with miscalculated date information.

As of June 1, 1998, not one of the 108 nuclear power plants in the United States was ready to perform reliably on January 1, 2000. Recently, the Nuclear Regulatory Commission issued a memo warning that numerous non safety-related, but important computer-based systems—primarily databases and data collection necessary for plant operations—are very dependent on time-sensitive calculations that are vulnerable to the Y2K problem.

Therefore, it is probable that many nuclear plants may be forced to shut down. Up to 20 percent of all North American electrical power is generated by nuclear reactors. A number of eastern states rely on these nuclear power plants for up to 45 percent of their electrical power. The loss of electricity from a forced shut down of these nuclear generating plants would result in brownouts and possibly blackouts, even if the rest of the hydro and coal generating plants remain online. A nuclear plant may contain as many as 300 different computer systems as well as embedded microchips that are potentially subject to Y2K.

Power Blackouts During the Ice Storm in 1998

Shortly after New Year's Day 1998, a massive ice storm wiped out vast portions of the power generating system that provides electricity to homes and businesses in the northeastern portion of North America. Although there was tremendous inconvenience, lost businesses, and some medical emergencies, the temperature did not drop toward -20° Celsius, which minimized the potential loss of life. The problem was eventually solved because the electrical power utilities in Quebec and Eastern Canada were able to call upon assistance from qualified utility crews throughout North America. But what will happen when almost every major power grid in North America and around the world simultaneously breaks down? Who can you call for assistance when everyone else is in the same crisis? In addition, during the ice storm blackout, to keep farms and some small businesses running, portable electrical power generators were purchased from across North America to keep minimal power going. Unfortunately, it soon became apparent that all of the portable generators available throughout the continent were quickly bought up, and no additional units were available, regardless of price.

Our entire global electrical power system is now dependent upon millions of embedded computer microchips. We know that some of these chips may fail, plunging our cities into darkness and cold during the dead of winter on January 1, 2000. According to reports by Dr. Gary North, at the end of May 1998 not one major power generating system in North America had declared that it is compliant and ready to operate properly in the new millennium.

The electrical power generating plants in the rest of the world have barely begun to work on the massive problem of getting ready for the year 2000. We know that most computer programming projects are completed late and generally cost more than expected; moreover, they usually fail to perform as expected. Therefore, one can conclude that it is almost impossible that the enormously complex Y2K computer project will be completed without error and on time to meet the January 1, 2000 deadline.

In light of the foregoing analysis, you may conclude that your small business, ministry, or home may likely be without electrical power for some period of time following the beginning of the next millennium. This period of blackout may last a few days, or a few months. While some commentators warn of an electrical power blackout lasting for many months, or possibly a year, I believe that the resourcefulness and abilities of the technicians will find solutions that will have most of the essential power grid in North America back up and running, despite occasional disruptions, within a matter of weeks or a few months, at worst. If we do lose our electricity for a period of time, the effects on our personal and business lives may be extraordinary. The loss of electricity for any significant period of time will most probably close businesses, banks, and government agencies.

Personal Electrical Power Generation

You may conclude, after personally researching the Y2K vulnerabilities of the electrical power system in your local area, that the risks of losing electricity for a significant period of time are very high. If this is your conclusion, you may want to consider buying a portable electrical power generator that will provide the essential electricity for your home or small business. For approximately $3200 you can purchase an eight-kilowatt diesel fuel electrical power generator that will run for up to 50,000 hours, which amounts to between twelve and fifteen years of normal usage. When you purchase such a generator, it will normally include a repair kit that will allow you to extend the useful life of the generator by another fifteen years. It is relatively simple at this time (if you act now) to acquire a generator and its necessary diesel fuel, plus the underground storage tanks to hold this fuel. The longer you wait to acquire such emergency equipment, the higher the price will rise until it may become practically impossible for the average home owner to acquire an electrical generator at any price. The ability to generate reliable electrical power during the first few months of the new millennium may protect your family and business, as well as provide desperately needed power to your neighbors.

Water and Sewage Utilities May Also Fail in 2000

Another example of the approaching Year 2000 problem is revealed in a report from Australia that indicates that their Coffs Harbor water-storage utility was subject to the Year 2000 bug when their programmers attempted to modify their computer software. When they tested it to see if it would perform properly after January 1, 2000, to the dismay of town officials the Y2K test showed that the computers, as they presently existed, would inadvertently trigger the dumping of a year's supply of chemicals into the water system. The test revealed that this Y2K computer error, if not corrected in time, would have killed almost every citizen of the town. In response to this Y2K wake-up call, Australian State Information Technology Minister Kim Yeadon issued orders to every one of Australia's four hundred government agencies to conduct tests and report on their exposure to the millennium virus by June 1998.

The Y2K Threat to Telecommunications

Many of the most progressive and profitable businesses in the world are involved in providing state of the art telecommunications that connect companies and governments around the world with instantaneous and reliable communications. Every business, government agency, and person in our modern world depends on the modern interconnected world of telecommunications to communicate with others. However, this world of satellites, fiber optic cables, T1 connections, faxes, telephones, modems, Internet, and e-mail is tremendously vulnerable to the millennium virus. While the companies that make up the telecommunications industry are desperately working around the clock to make sure that you will still have a dial tone on New Year's Day, 2000, there is a significant risk that at least some parts of the communications system may not work. It is extremely troubling that as of June 1, 1998, not one major telecommunications company in the world has announced that it is Year 2000–compliant, despite the obvious commercial advantages to any corporation that can prove that it has truly solved its internal Y2K problems.

One recent example of a telecommunications breakdown demonstrates the vulnerability of our worldwide communications network. A satellite called Galaxy IV developed computer problems at 6 P.M. on May 19, 1998, that prevented it from relaying pager messages and electronic media feeds. The satellite's onboard control system and backup switch failed, which caused the satellite to rotate out of its proper orbit. Within minutes, approximately 80 percent of the 40 million users of the pager system lost their service. The state police in New Hampshire lost the use of their major crimes unit's paging system for officers. In another state the satellite failure prevented customers from using their credit and debit cards at the pay-at-the-pump machines. While this temporary crisis was not caused by Y2K problems, it is an excellent example of how vulnerable we are to the failure of sophisticated computer systems.

How serious would it be if the telephones went down as we usher in the new millennium? Virtually everything in your life would come crashing down without a reliable telephone and communications system. The entire banking system depends upon instantaneous telephone communications for both voice and computer data transmission. It is responsible to connect our nation's banks with each other and the thousands of banks and millions of customers throughout the globe. The entire universe of stock trading and bond investing depends on immediate telephone communications. Without reliable telecommunications, the banks and stock market would grind to a halt, triggering the loss of billions of dollars. Computer expert Peter de Jager warns, "If we lose the ability to make a phone call, then we lose everything. We lose electronic fund transfers, we lose trading, we lose branch-banking."

A report on the risk to our phone communications recently appeared in *USA Today* on May 20, 1998 entitled, "Year 2000 Bug Threatens Phone Service." Lou Marcoccio, a research director on telecommunications with the Gartner Group, warned that, despite the billions of dollars spent on fixing Y2K, we face at least a 50 percent risk that major phone companies may succumb to significant failures of their mission critical systems. The Federal Communications Commission has admitted that the millennium virus may negatively impact critical services including fire, police, and paramedic dispatch systems. Michael Powell, the FCC Commissioner, warned that at the present time "the vast majority of police and fire equipment is not Year 2000 compliant." In light of the constant battles such departments must fight to survive with their existing budgets, it is doubtful that every critical service will correct its computers in time to meet the deadline.

The *USA Today* article reported that the Gartner Group's research found that the largest U.S. telecommunications carriers are spending between $70 million and $400 million each to correct their Y2K problem. For example, the largest telecommunication giant, AT&T, will spend $463 million on its computers, spread over two years (according to AT&T's spokesman John Pasqua). Another large firm, SBC Communications Group, announced that it will spend more than $250 million to get its computers ready for the year 2000. The experts warn that small and mid-size telecommunications firms are the most likely to have noncompliant systems. In addition, communications utilities in Europe, Asia, and South America are far behind the North American utilities in responding to the Year 2000 challenge.

It is possible that the worst Y2K problems will show up in the area of billings. For example, if you make a phone call to your mother at 11:59 P.M. on December 31, 1999 and converse for fifteen minutes into the New Year, you might be shocked to receive your monthly telephone bill in February for $1,795,505. Some telephone billing computers might not recognize "00," and mistakenly bill you for a ninety-nine-year long-distance call (from 1900 to 1999).

Notes

1. Cowles, Rick. "EUY2K.com. – Electric Utilities and Year 2000," Internet.
2. *Business Week*, March 1998.
3. Ibid.

6

The Coming Banking and Insurance Company Crisis

The Enormous Cost of Fixing the Banks' Computer Systems

Could the Year 2000 computer bug destroy your bank's computer system and endanger both your life savings and your company's financial well-being? History reveals that our entire worldwide financial structure is built on the public's confidence in the rock-solid reliability of the banking system. When hundreds of millions of people entrust their precious life savings to their local bankers, they do so because they have come to believe that their money is safer in the vaults of their city's bank than it would be in a strongbox or a safe inside their own home. However, the quickly approaching deadline of the beginning of the new millennium is likely to severely test that assumption.

The evidence I have gathered over the last year presents a bleak picture of the Year 2000 readiness of the nation's banking system, and, indeed, the international banking system as a whole. The significance of the problem is very difficult to overestimate. Every aspect of everyone's life will be negatively impacted if our banking system finds itself unable to operate properly in the year 2000. A failure of your bank's computer systems would imperil its ability to transfer your funds, cash your checks, and operate the ATMs that give you access to your cash. This failure, in turn, could imperil the essential bank credit needed to allow companies and businesses to operate and pay their employees on time. Moreover, the failure of the international banking system for any period of time could result in massive worldwide unemployment and the collapse of most essential government operations.

How would the governments around the world collect their essential taxes or pay their civil servants and soldiers, let alone pay their suppliers of goods and services, if the banking system cannot clear the hundreds of millions of daily financial transactions that allow the whole economy to function smoothly? Literally trillions of dollars of credits, debits, checks, and electronic transactions are processed every day by a truly awesome and incredibly complex system of interconnected computers and clearinghouse transaction centers. A breakdown in any of these intricately connected computer systems would almost certainly spread immediately throughout the global financial system, triggering the worst, most devastating banking collapse in history.

An article in *The Sunday Times* of London newspaper outlined the scope of the banking industry's Year 2000 problems in these words from a banking computer expert: "This is not a prediction. It is a certainty—there will be serious disruption in the world's financial services industry. I can't tell whether it's going to be 10 percent business failure, or a meltdown, but it's going to be ugly. It will start with a millennium-induced crash of the world's stock markets around the middle of 1999."[1] Investment counselor Tony Keyes provided another view on the problem: "The crash of 1929 will pale in comparison to the 'crash of the century.' Layoffs will be rampant, unemployment will rise dramatically, and the economy will drown in dismal depression."[2]

Do the major banks believe this crisis will seriously affect their operations? Considering the well-known aversion of banks to spend any of their profits on anything that is not absolutely essential for their continued success, the following examples of the awesome sums being invested by major banks to fix their computers should demonstrate persuasively that we are facing a tremendous crisis. For example, the Chase-Manhattan Bank, one of the largest in the world, will spend more than $250 million to correct the date problems within its computers before the Year 2000 deadline. Alan Greenspan, the reticent Chairman of the Federal Reserve, has admitted the danger is real in his testimony to the U.S. Senate subcommittee, in response to a question by Senator Bennett (Utah): "Inevitable difficulties are going to emerge. . . . You could end up with . . . a very large problem."

Recently, newspapers reported that federal and Georgia state banking regulators imposed strict sanctions on a bank in Eatonton, Georgia, whose owners had failed to correct the bank's Y2K computer problems. The *American Banker* magazine wrote an article that revealed details about the investigation of the Eatonton bank in Georgia. The fact that this was publicized in a banking magazine suggests that its purpose was to bring a wake-up call to the banking industry throughout America.

Regulators last week fired a shot across the bow of the banking industry as it sails toward the turn-of-the-century deadline for getting its computer systems in shape. For the first time, regulators cracked down on a bank that they said has not done enough to ensure its computers were ready for 2000. . . . The Federal Reserve Board hit . . . (the Eatonton bank in Georgia) . . . with a cease-and-desist order that requires (it) to repair its systems and report its progress frequently under a strict series of deadlines. The Federal Deposit Insurance Corporation and the Georgia Department of Banking issued similar enforcement actions against the company's three subsidiary banks. . . . Lawmakers are putting the heat on the agencies to take action, industry observers said.

The disaster throughout our society, if the banking system fails, is hard to comprehend. If our banking systems collapse, then it may be virtually impossible for most companies to operate. They would not be able to pay their employees, suppliers, or service providers (such as utility companies). Without the ability to confidently cash the checks of their customers, they could not stay in business. How will the government collect taxes or pay its own employees, police, and soldiers? Will your home in the city be safe if welfare checks cannot be delivered or cashed and if most stores are forced to close because customers have no ability to pay for purchases? Dr. Leon Kappelman, co-chairman of the Year 2000 Working Group of the Society for Information Management, commented on the risks to our society from the failure of the banking system to fix their computers in time, "This is potentially the most destructive part of the year 2000 problem. This isn't the inconvenience part where your paycheck comes a few days late. This is the blood-in-the-streets part."[3]

I do not want to be an alarmist, but the very possibility of this scenario coming to pass should cause any reader to carefully consider the possible risks to his home and family if the worst happens and these critical systems fail. Always remember that although the crisis is real, it is only temporary. Humans are incredibly innovative in finding solutions to desperate problems. I expect that after a few months of chaos, dedicated government and corporate programmers working around the clock on emergency repairs will solve the worst of the computer problems. However, during the initial months, those who have understood the dangers and have taken preventative measures will be prepared to protect their family and friends from the dangers that will follow the potential breakdowns.

What Are Bankers Saying about the Y2K Problem?

One of the first major media articles on the Year 2000 crisis appeared in *Newsweek* magazine on June 2, 1997. It discussed the approaching banking crisis in the following terms:

> Banks and other financial institutions will generally go bonkers if they don't fix their problem. . . . In the worst case scenario, the entire financial infrastructure, including the stock market, will go haywire. Balances, records, and transactions will be lost. . . . Y2K could be the event that could all but paralyze the planet. . . . Forget about a silver bullet. It seems that in most mainframe programs, dates appear more often than M*A*S*H reruns on television— about once in every 50 lines of code, with many computers containing millions, if not tens of millions, of lines. Typically, it's hard to find those particular lines, because the original programs, often written in the ancient COBOL computer language, are quirky and undocumented."[4]

After ignoring the Y2K problem for many years, the business magazines have finally acknowledged that this crisis will affect nearly every corporation in the world. *Business Week* broke the conspiracy of silence in the corporate world in its article on the Year 2000 crisis in its August 12, 1996 issue. The article warned that the financial world "is especially vulnerable." This responsible journal raised the specter of "a global financial meltdown" as the writer warned of the growing dangers that the "clearing and settlement of transactions could break down. Stocks held electronically [might be] wiped out. Interest might not be properly credited." Finally, the article warned, "Deposits or trades might not be credited to an account." In what was almost an understatement in light of the aforementioned warnings, the *Business Week* article warned that the "consequences may be catastrophic."[5]

An article in *The Sunday Times* of London discussed the impending dangers to the economy from the banking industry's failure to fix its computers on time.

> According to the latest research from three of Wall Street's biggest investment banks, the [Y2K] problem could damage New York's financial industry by disabling those banks or brokerage firms that are not prepared for the change. Merril Lynch, which has a $200 million budget to tackle the problem, says it "poses a genuine challenge to the networked world." Morgan Stanley, which is spending $60 million, describes it as "a serious and critical challenge for all modern organizations." Goldman Sachs says the problem has "far reaching implications, not just for the computing services industries, but for all businesses."[6]

William McDonnough, the president of the New York Federal Reserve Bank, made the following statement about the dangers: "Getting the Year 2000 issue right is critical for every organization. Failure to get it right will effect the integrity of the payments system and the performance of the domestic, and maybe even the global economy."

The problems in other nations such as South Africa are even worse than those facing America and Canada. Elmer Roberg, the president of Business Transformation Services in South Africa, said the following: "The Year 2000 software problem . . . is likely to be the greatest challenge ever faced by the world economy. Its size, scope, and solution, as well as the immovability of its end date, are likely to show that it will be one of the most complex projects ever undertaken by mankind." Another expert, Mr. Robert Lau, the managing consultant at PA Consulting in Hong Kong, has issued the following estimate of the dangers to the global banking system: "It is our prediction that it will only take 5 to 10 percent of the world's bank payments' systems to not work on that one day to create a global liquidity lock-up. . . . I don't think the markets have quite grasped the implications of what will happen if the entire system goes down."[7]

The danger to the banking system is so overwhelming that major banks such as Citicorp are expending vast sums to solve their Y2K problem before it destroys the U.S. banking system. A report from *USA Today* on June 10, 1998 suggests that Citicorp will spend an astonishing $600 million to fix their computer systems. BankAmerica has more than a thousand programmers working full time to solve their Y2K problems at a cost exceeding $380 million. We need to recognize that in the global economy today, no bank and, therefore, no individual is isolated from the others. We are all interconnected in a complex system that imperils every other system if one member fails to correct its Y2K computer problems before the January 1, 2000 deadline.

On February 18, 1998, the *Wall Street Journal* ran a front-page article entitled, "Help Wanted: The IRS Searches for a World Class Computer Wizard." The article indicated that the government's top official charged with correcting the Year 2000 problem for the Internal Revenue Service, Chief Information Officer Arthur Gross, resigned to accept a better opportunity in the business sector. The article described that the IRS commissioner, Charles Rossotti, recently hired an executive headhunter to locate a replacement for Mr. Gross. The article suggested that "Mr. Gross's successor will face the biggest technology management challenge in the world." This is not an overstatement. The *Wall Street Journal* article added, "Finding a replacement for Mr. Gross won't be easy . . . when you get to work for the IRS at half the pay or less than you'll get in the private sector."[8]

Interviews with key players in the banking, accounting, and stock brokering industries provide ample evidence that these industries have decided to limit the information that they will provide to their customers, or the public, because of their concern that this information may damage their business and possibly lead to future lawsuits. Therefore, you can expect to hear mostly positive information in the press releases from these industries, information is carefully written by their legal staff to provide protection from the coming deluge of Year 2000 lawsuits.

The Euro Conversion and Y2K Threaten Europe

In Europe, bankers have focused almost all of their attention and computer programming resources on getting the European Union ready for the January 1, 1999 deadline for the conversion of all major European currencies to the new common euro. It is proving to be a massive computer programming challenge that is far exceeding their initial estimates in terms of both time and cost. However, a very disturbing additional cost of the euro conversion is that it is nearly impossible for European banks, insurance companies, and government agencies to simultaneously convert their massive computer systems to solve the Y2K problem.

After all but ignoring the growing dangers posed to European financial stability by the Y2K problem, the leading central bankers and ministers of finance of the G-10 (a group representing the ten leading industrial nations) have finally awakened to the approaching catastrophe. An urgent meeting on this crisis was held on September 9, 1997 in Basel, Switzerland. They issued this communiqué about the potential for a huge international banking crisis that could collapse the entire financial system: "The year 2000 issue is potentially the biggest challenge ever faced by the financial industry. Weak links could pose a risk even to banks and businesses whose computer systems are functioning smoothly."

The governors of the central banks of the G-10 group of Ten Nations published a "Year 2000 Compliance" statement to alert all of the world's banks, securities firms, and stock markets to the growing danger. "It is possible, in the light of the enormous scale and range of financial market participants, that certain applications may fail to operate smoothly on January 1, 2000. It is therefore important that all financial institutions, and in particular market bodies such as exchanges and clearing houses, develop appropriate contingency plans to deal with any interruptions to counterparty trades and payments."

Several months later (Nov. 18, 1997), the Basel Committee on Banking Supervision also issued a statement on the growing size and urgency of the Y2K problem: "This issue carries tremendous risks of disruption in the operation of financial institutions and in financial markets. The aim is to encourage financial institutions worldwide to commit urgently the resources necessary to become millennium compliant in a timely fashion."

The banks in the United States have actively encouraged their customers, including the government, to take advantage of the automated deposit systems that bypass paper checks in favor of direct deposit of funds into personal bank accounts. This Automated Clearinghouse connects over three dozen regional clearinghouses together in a nationwide network that handles 3.5 billion checks or automatic direct deposits annually. This represents an incredible $11 trillion per year. This awesomely complex automated deposit system instantly connects more than a thousand federal agencies together with the agencies of all fifty individual state governments. Added to this system are another twenty thousand financial corporations including banks, savings and loans, credit unions, and over half a million corporations. The vulnerability of this complex system to the approaching Year 2000 crisis is potentially catastrophic.

If the banks' computers are not corrected in time, you may find that your bank will send you a statement in February 2000 demanding hundreds of thousands of dollars of back interest payments and penalties because their computer thinks you have missed making payments on your car loan for over a hundred years. If the bank's computers fail, how will you gain access to your life savings and how will you verify your account balance? Will your bank be able to cash your employer's paycheck when thousands of other bank customers are demanding their funds in cash?

An article on the Internet by Robert Winnett of *The Sunday Times* of London reported that a senior bank executive of Barclays Bank in the United Kingdom has warned of the dangers of the Year 2000 computer crisis. He advises people to acquire real currency, to buy gold and silver coins, and to possibly sell their real estate to protect their family in the face of the coming Year 2000 crisis. Winnett continued, "The average man or woman does not appreciate what is going to happen. . . I'm going to prepare for the absolute worst—I'm talking about the need to start buying candles, tinned food, and bottled water from the mid-1999 onwards. People think that I am mad, but a company director I met last week is intending to set up a commune and buy a shotgun because the potential for looting is also quite high." Winnett reports that even a senior executive of the Midland Bank, who has concluded that the problems of the Y2K crisis will impact all of our bank accounts, suggests that "gold wouldn't be a bad thing to get into."[9]

A Bank Holiday May Be Coming to Your Bank

Even before we arrive at January 1, 2000, the growing awareness of the dangers that Y2K pose to our banking system may cause millions of citizens to decide they might be wise to withdraw their funds from their bank accounts until they see that all is well with their local banks. Few people realize how little cash actually exists in our "cashless" society today. Many think of the cashless society as something that may occur at some point in the future. However, the dangerous reality is that the government mints have produced paper currency and coins equal to only 3 percent of the total currency that governments, corporations, and individuals have accumulated in their various bank accounts.

Our North American banking system is known as a "fractional reserve system," one in which the government demands that the banks keep a very small amount of their customer's deposits in their vaults. Normally, 3 percent is sufficient because every time someone wants their money in cash, another customer comes into the bank to deposit their cash receipts. Typically, it all balances out.

The Y2K Run on the Banks

However, if the banking run begins during the 1999 panic, due to the Y2K crisis, this 3 percent cash reserve will be inadequate. Despite valiant attempts to fly containers of newly printed bank notes from the twelve regional Federal Reserve Banks to the affected banks, the demand may quickly outstrip the supply of cash in a matter of days, if not hours. When that day arrives— when, not if—those few wise individuals who have prudently turned their stocks, bonds, and bank accounts into hard cash, gold, and silver may be the only people in the country who will have economic options. On that day, "Cash will be king."

The implications of the fact that banks don't have all of the money people deposit in their accounts may begin to dawn on millions of people as the growing computer breakdowns are increasingly publicized. If only 5 percent of the bank's depositors demand to withdraw their life savings in cash, the banks will be forced to close the tellers' windows and their empty vaults. Obviously, the Federal Reserve will desperately try to resupply a local bank that is experiencing a bank run, but there is only a limited amount of paper currency in reserve.

What will the government and the banks do when the lineups begin, sometime in 1999 when a significant minority of depositors and corporate customers become aware of the extent of the Y2K problem and begin to fear that immediate access to their funds may be imperiled? Obviously, the first step may be for the national governments to place severe legal limitations on the cash withdrawals allowed per day or per month. Then the government may begin to print paper currency in huge amounts to try to meet the demand and stop the bank runs. Some confidential sources have told me privately that the U.S. Federal Reserve system, the comptroller of the currency, and their counterparts in other nations have already printed massive amounts of paper currency that is available when the banking runs begin. However, even this may be insufficient to stem the tide. If the banks collapse, this may lead to a collapse in the international banking system, and the global capital markets that are tied into it would collapse as customers succumb to panic.

The banking industry has already worked out plans with the government to buy some time for the banks by declaring a bank holiday, or moratorium, for a limited period of time. In the United States, a federal law known as the Monetary Control Act of 1980 sets the stage for the government to declare a series of bank holidays that will effectively protect the banks from the onslaught of desperate customers who are frantic to get their hands on the cash they mistakenly believed would always be available.

The Monetary Control Act of 1980 - Section 705 (2) (b) (1)

The act reads as follows:

In the event of a natural calamity, riot, insurrection, war, or other emergency conditions occurring in any State whether caused by acts of nature or man, the Comptroller of the Currency may designate by proclamation any day a legal holiday for the national banking associations located in that State. In the event that the emergency conditions affect only part of a State, the Comptroller of the Currency may designate the part so affected and may proclaim a legal holiday for the national banking associations located in an affected part.

Please note the precise wording in this act—"or other emergency conditions occurring in any State whether caused by acts of nature or man." This act gives the federal government the power to shut the doors of any bank in America, preventing the depositors from getting access to their hard-earned cash. When the runs on the banks begin, the government may proclaim these bank holidays for as long as it is deemed necessary to protect these essential financial institutions and to stop depositors from emptying the bank vaults.

In addition to declaring a bank holiday, another option the government may choose during the coming financial panic is to create monetary regulations that will provide for a thirty-day (or longer) waiting period for depositors to get their cash.

Even if most of the banks and corporations manage to correct their computers before the millennium deadline, they may be unable to transact normal electronic communications and exchange computer data with companies who are not Y2K-compliant, including entire foreign nations or economic regions. This necessary triage choice of cutting off communications with noncompliant regions and financial corporations may trigger an economic and financial implosion that may result in a massive contraction in global trading. This problem is inevitable. The clock is running, and the countdown cannot be stopped.

Goldman Sachs, one of the world's most respected and powerful investment bankers, has declared that "the combined computer expertise in all of Europe was not enough to fix that continent's problems in time, even if all those programmers quit their present jobs and worked on nothing but Y2K from now on." When considering the nature of this crisis, it is critical to realize that it is impossible to solve this problem, in the diminishing time that remains, by throwing additional computer programmers or money at it. Anyone who has been part of a complex computer software upgrade knows that simply hiring additional programmers or increasing the budget will actually tend to delay the successful completion date even further (and also could tend to produce additional computer programming errors and bugs because of the confusion and haste). Nick Edwards, a computer banking consultant who has studied the impact of this problem extensively, has written, "The millennium bug computer crisis threatens a global liquidity lock-up that could send the world financial markets crashing."[10]

Computer expert Walt Lamphere gives the following warning:

> Every person that begins to understand the enormity of the disaster looming on the horizon will contribute to growing awareness. But, who will leave his or her money in the bank, when it may be impossible to get your money the next day, or next week. Who will not join the rush? Will you leave your money in your bank if there is more than a good chance you will not have access to it, due to computer lock up?

He also comments on the value of having at least some gold and silver in your survival portfolio.

> I suspect the value of hard currency will also be greatly enhanced in the near future. Gold and silver have been historically the haven of those concerned with retention of value of their money.

Y2K Banking: A Credit Crisis

President Thomas Jefferson warned in 1799, "Banking establishments are more dangerous than standing armies." In the Great Depression of the 1930s, a huge number of banks failed because of their exposure to bad investments in real estate, non-paying loans, and massive withdrawals by their customers. More than 4,700 banks failed between 1928 and 1932. As a result of this crisis, President Roosevelt proclaimed a bank moratorium on March 6, 1933, leaving millions of Americans without access to their cash. While some people later received a portion of their funds, many others lost everything they had deposited.

Will Federal Deposit Insurance Protect Your Savings?

The U.S. Congress responded to these bank failures by establishing an insurance system to guarantee the funds deposited by bank customers. The Federal Deposit Insurance Corporation (FDIC), created in 1933, now insures bank deposits up to $100,000 per customer for member banks. In Canada, bank deposits are insured up to $60,000. However, not all banks are insured. Since it is a voluntary system, over five hundred U.S. banks are not insured by the FDIC. Member banks have a sign on the door proclaiming their membership in FDIC. However, during the recent savings and loan crisis, the FDIC was overwhelmed with claims. This failure forced the federal government to directly bail out the S&L system at a cost of $700 billion. Despite the warning signs from the savings and loan collapse, the Federal Deposit Insurance Corporation remains disastrously underfunded.

Today the FDIC has assets of approximately $1 billion to insure the bank deposits of over fourteen thousand banks and S&L accounts of all Americans. This amounts to $4 trillion at risk. Less than two and a half cents of FDIC assets insure every hundred dollars of insured bank deposits! Knowledgeable sources warn that thousands of banks are dangerously exposed through their failure to make correcting their Year 2000 computer problems a number-one priority.

When the Federal Reserve finally raised the Y2K warning in early 1998, it was too late for many banks to find, repair, and properly test their complex computer systems before the new millennium. The consequences of this colossal management failure may devastate these banks, their customers, employees, and communities. The present insolvency of the FDIC makes it possible that millions may lose their life savings in a future bank collapse.

Edward Yardeni, the chief economist of Deutsche Morgan Grenfell bank in New York, warns that the danger of a worldwide recession triggered by the Year 2000 computer crisis has risen to 60 percent. He has suggested that the damage to the U.S. economy may exceed $300 billion as the new millennium begins. Other experts on the impact of Y2K, such as Dr. Paul Bailes (Australia), have suggested that dislocation of the global economy caused by the Year 2000 computer virus may equal the devastation of the Great Depression.

As a basic principle, you should plan to diversify your savings and investments in light of the growing dangers to the whole financial system posed by the Y2K crisis. At some point in 1999, the risk of a bank collapse may trigger a huge run on the banks somewhere in the world. This news could motivate a growing number of people to begin to withdraw their funds in fear that they might lose their life savings. Those who come to that decision first will safely withdraw their money. However, those who wait too long may find that the banks have either closed or the government has declared a bank holiday for a period of time. I cannot tell you the precise moment to withdraw some of your funds. That is a judgment call you must make for yourself. However, in light of the known fact that approximately 3 percent of the nation's money actually exists as paper currency or coins, it is obvious that it will be impossible for the banks or the government to provide enough currency to satisfy even a small percentage of the banks' customers. Should you withdraw all of your savings as cash or just enough to provide for three to six months of purchases of food, gas, and other essentials until the worst of the possible Year 2000 crisis is resolved? Unless this crisis brings about the total collapse of the banking system, which is unlikely, many may choose to withdraw only enough to pay for necessary purchases for a period of months. Between now and the time when you choose to withdraw cash, you probably should not deposit more than $50,000 in any one bank. Place your life savings in several different banks after you have verified, through one of the bank-rating services, that the bank is financially sound. In 1999, some banks and stock brokers will begin to advertise that they are "Year 2000-compliant." It may be wise to move your savings into a Y2K-compliant bank at that time to minimize the risk to your family, business, or church.

The Y2K Problems of the Insurance Industry

Although insurance companies were among the first to address the Y2K problem, the *Statistical Abstract of the United States* reveals that they hold investments of over $3 trillion in the form of government T-bills and real estate investments, and over $1.5 trillion in stock market investments. This staggering amount of money invested by the insurance industry in equities and bonds gives us an indication of the vulnerability of our entire financial system to the computer problems that may affect almost every computer system in the world.

Despite starting as early as 1989, many insurance companies are playing catch-up as they try to bring their huge computer systems into Year 2000 compliance. For example, Prudential Life Insurance Co. will spend $120 million to fix its systems. On June 10, 1998, *The Toronto Star* newspaper reported that an insurance company, Unum Corporation, miscalculated the year 2000 as 1900 and inadvertently canceled thousands of policies. When Phillips Petroleum Company ran a simulated Year 2000 test on the computers that control the sophisticated safety systems that detect dangerous gases such as hydrogen sulfide gas (that occasionally erupt from the oil wells deep beneath the ocean in the North Sea), the computers promptly shut down entirely, endangering the whole drilling platform.

Lloyds of London, the world's greatest insurance syndicate, has been advised by its computer insurance specialists that they face enormous risk exposure in light of the Year 2000 catastrophe. Their top experts warned that "they should anticipate paying out upwards of $800 billion to $1 trillion in litigation expenses." Maurice Newman, the chairman of the Australian Year 2000 Steering Committee, stated in a speech, "Lloyds underwriters are already withdrawing cover from airlines and air safety regulatory authorities if their situation is unsatisfactory."

Will People Trust Computers after January 1, 2000?

As we all know, every aspect of our modern society is now dependent on complex computer calculations that, until now, we have all trusted. However, a critical question is now raised by the approaching Y2K computer crisis: Will the millions of people around the globe continue to complacently trust in the accuracy of computers after the beginning of the new millennium? It is entirely possible that hundreds of millions of people will strongly reject the computer systems of the new millennium in light of their proven failure to correctly calculate dates and transactions that spanned the century crossover.

Psychological studies and personal research reveal that a significant minority of people in our modern society are deeply distrustful of computers and the revolution in information technology that has invaded our lives in the last five decades. Many people seriously question whether computers are worth the price in either dollars, or lost jobs, produced by the wholesale acceptance of new computer technology by both industry and government. While experts proclaim that computer technology produces more jobs than it destroys, there is no question that millions of individuals have suffered personally as computers have made their jobs obsolete. Millions of people have experienced the effects of computer errors and systems failures and are now distrustful of placing their lives or their job under the control of these sometimes temperamental computer systems.

For example, the London Ambulance Service that provides essential paramedical services to the millions of citizens in the British capital experienced a computer breakdown that imperiled essential life-saving services when it was introduced. The management of the London government agency decided to expend almost $20 million to develop a sophisticated computer system that would replace their existing reliable system of human dispatchers to answer emergency calls and direct the ambulances to the needy citizen, by the most efficient route calculated by the computer. When the complex and sophisticated system went online, a communications disaster occurred. The system made it impossible for emergency calls to get through for the first day and a half. Then the new system began charting creative new routes across the vast city of London that resulted in ambulances failing to get their patients to the hospital emergency rooms in time to save their lives. The remaining staff finally prevailed upon management to close down the deadly new system and restore the old-fashioned, but extremely reliable, human dispatchers, who knew the byways of their city like the back of their hands. The expensive new system was never tried again.

This is one of hundreds of examples I could cite of new sophisticated computer systems failing to operate as promised. Unfortunately, these notorious computer failures are just a foretaste of the greatest computer failure in history that is coming to a computer near you, on January 1, 2000.

Other studies note that, despite the expenditure of over $1 trillion dollars since 1970 on computer technology around the world, the economists have found that, to their surprise, the level of growth in productivity which grew rapidly after World War II began to slow in the 1970s, despite vast expenditures on computer hardware and software. While it is obvious that many businesses and government agencies could not prosper or even function without modern computer technology, many people doubt that our wholesale acceptance of computers has been an entirely beneficial event for humanity.

Possibly the disaster that will afflict millions of computers throughout the globe following January 1, 2000, may lead to a sober reappraisal of the pros and cons of accepting every single computer technological advance without considering carefully its impact on the quality of life of those affected by the new system. It is certainly possible that many will be unwilling to voluntarily submit to placing their lives under the control of future computer systems if there is any viable alternative.

Notes

1. *The Sunday Times* of London, August 3, 1997.
2. Keyes, Tony. *Computer World,* October 27, 1997.
3. Kappelman, Leon.
4. "The Day The World Shuts Down," *Newsweek*, June 2, 1997.
5. *Business Week*, August 12, 1996.
6. *The Sunday Times* of London, August 3, 1997.
7. *Reuters*, October 1, 1997.
8. *Wall Street Journal*, February, 18, 1998.
9. Winnett, Robert. *The Sunday Times* of London, March 29, 1998.
10. *Reuters,* October 1, 1997.

7

The Dangers of a Y2K Stock Market Collapse

Nervous investors throughout the world will begin to appreciate the gravity of the Year 2000 crisis in the coming months as they read about the growing number of computer crashes that may afflict many corporations and government agencies long before the year 2000. Many investors may begin to suspect that the staggering costs of repairing millions of lines of computer code and the growing realization of the risk of huge Y2K lawsuits may negatively affect the profits of major corporations for the next few years. The government and the accounting profession have ruled that companies must write off the cost of Y2K repairs in the year these costs were incurred, rather than spread them over several years. Additionally, the fear that the Y2K crisis may adversely affect the complex computer systems that connect the stock exchange to stockbrokers may cause many overvalued share prices to plummet long before the year 2000.

Because of the impending Year 2000 crisis, we face the risk of the greatest stock market crash since 1929. Meanwhile, millions of naive, inexperienced investors are pouring their life savings into arrays of newly formed mutual funds. Over thirty million new investors placed their savings into the stock market during the last four years. Stocks and mutual funds are now at the highest levels anyone has ever seen. The dangers today are far greater than they were in 1929. Today, a huge portion of the average family's financial assets is invested in the stock market. The 1929 meltdown of the stock market did not immediately lead to a worldwide collapse of other stock markets because national markets were not integrated then. Few multinational companies were traded on multiple national stock markets early in this century.

Today our global stock and bond markets are so completely integrated that markets in Hong Kong or Europe react instantly to a crisis in New York. The recent financial crisis in South Korea and Indonesia immediately sent a shock wave through stock markets in Europe and in North America. A major crash on Wall Street or on the London Exchange would trigger an instant worldwide financial collapse. Additionally, the complex system of interconnected computers that ties the entire world's financial system into one network exposes every connected party to the danger that the millennium virus could be transmitted from noncompliant computers to Y2K-compliant computers, causing even the compliant computers to crash.

The North American stock markets are already at risk of entering a major bear market. Historians of the stock market warn that a century of analysis reveals that long-term bull markets, such as America has been experiencing since 1989, almost inevitably end with a spectacular blow-off and a brutal bear market, which could potentially destroy the life savings of tens of millions of people. During the thirty months that followed the initial 1929 crash, American share prices fell 89 percent. The stock market crash and the brutal bear market that followed wiped out $85 billion. Although stock investors suffered major initial losses when the crash first occurred, the market continued to fall for the next several years. Investors who abandoned the market after taking their first beating were saved from worse losses that followed. Many investors rode the market all the way to the bottom and were nearly wiped out. A fundamental rule of investing: your first loss is your best loss. Analyze your loss, learn the lesson, and get out.

The speculative mania that has overtaken the U.S. stock market in the last few years is now moving into global markets. However, a majority of these investors are new to the stock market. Many are naive and unaware of the tremendous dangers of a bear market. In 1988, 34 million Americans were invested in the stock market. In only ten years, this number has risen to 75 million. More than half of these investors are placing their money in the stock market for the first time, often through one of the eight thousand mutual funds. In 1987, the mutual funds held $180 billion in equities. Eleven years later these mutual funds have grown to a staggering $2.5 trillion worth of stocks and bonds. Since the early 1990s investors have withdrawn almost a trillion dollars from their federally insured, low-interest, safe bank accounts and transferred these funds into the most speculative stock market in history. Over the last few years, an average of $11 billion was withdrawn from bank accounts every single month and reinvested in the stock market.

An unprecedented tidal wave of new money has poured into the market, naturally causing the price of shares to rise to previously unheard-of highs. Over 80 percent of the money now invested in mutual funds has been invested in the last four years. Therefore, most of these new mutual fund investors have bought stocks whose values are at the highest levels in the stock market's history. The risk of financial disaster for many investors is growing; their exposure to the stock and bond markets has grown astronomically.

When the stock markets begin to crash, it may be almost impossible to sell stocks or redeem mutual fund units; everyone else may be trying to bail out at the same time. After the collapse, when share prices have dropped to a fraction of their current prices, the smart money will begin buying up the market at bargain-basement prices. However, at that point, many investors may find that their life savings have all but vanished.

Many large banks and insurance companies are exposed to the potential of devastating losses from the risks of Y2K computer collapses, as well as the risks of Y2K lawsuits by shareholders and customers. These banks and insurance companies now hold well over $1 trillion dollars worth of equities and bonds, purchased at high prices in the last few years. When the financial losses from the Year 2000 virus hit the banks and insurance companies, many of these institutions may be forced to sell large amounts of their investment portfolios to raise liquid funds. These massive sales of stocks and bonds may place further downward pressure on prices and contribute to the sell-off.

When the 70 million Americans who own over $2 trillion in stocks and mutual funds begin to see that the stock market is crashing, a huge panic may sweep the country. It is unlikely that these new investors will "bite the bullet" and ride out their mounting losses. As stock prices plummet, many investors may attempt to pull their life savings out of the market—too late—to avoid shattering losses. Those who were prudent enough to move their funds out of the stock market and mutual funds long before the Year 2000 crisis-induced financial panic will not lose their funds, nor their ability to sleep soundly.

The Danger of Y2K and the Financial Derivatives Market

If all of the other banking-system Y2K computer problems were not sufficient to threaten the international financial system, consider the problems posed by the enormous new market known as financial derivative contracts. Derivative contracts are financial investment contracts whose value is "derived" from an underlying financial security such as a stock, bond, or a stock exchange index. The concept of derivatives is centuries old, existing, primarily, in the form of option contracts and futures contracts on the price of grain, or pigs' bellies, for example. These derivative contracts provide a significant economic function by allowing a farmer to lock in the final selling price of his corn crop in September at the time he plants the crop in April. This removes the risk of a change in the price of corn, which could destroy his profits. Some other investor is willing to bet that the price of corn will be some particular amount in September and will take that risk, hoping that the prevailing market price in September will actually be higher than the contract price he has guaranteed. Such option and future contracts even out the risks and provide a needed balancing function in the world of economics for many commodities.

However, in the last two decades, Wall Street stockbrokers and large banks have created an abundance of new, highly leveraged, speculative financial contracts called derivatives. Beginning with real estate investment trusts, the brokers created junk bonds, leveraged buyouts, options, and securitized debt. These bewildering, new, complex derivative contracts are so complicated that few people outside the actual computer wizards that design such derivative contracts truly understand their complexities or the risk to the investor. These derivatives are sold to major corporations and investors by brokers who sell the idea of massive profits if the contract goes their client's way, but who also often understate the staggering losses that will be endured if the derivative contract goes against the client. During the last decade, investors who failed to understand the total risk of the derivative contracts they had entered into with their banks or stockbrokers have lost billions of dollars. Meanwhile, the huge banks and stockbrokers were earning high commissions on these derivatives, regardless of how the trade actually worked out.

These more speculative, creative, and highly leveraged investments, designed to create staggering profits for their Wall Street brokers at great risk to the investor, are so speculative and dangerous that they could trigger the greatest economic collapse in history. Unlike normal direct investments in stocks and bonds, these new financial derivatives are totally artificial financial contracts. Derivatives can include such diverse financial vehicles as interest rate swaps and options, currency futures and options, stock index futures and options, collateralized mortgage obligations, commodity futures, and Eurodollar futures contracts. However, they are so highly leveraged that a one percent rise in the value of the underlying security may produce a 100 percent gain in the equity invested. However, a mere one percent decline could totally wipe out the investment.

Aside from the inherently risky nature of such speculative investments, the danger is multiplied when you consider the near certainty that massive computer errors and crashes may devastate the computer-driven derivatives market as we enter the new millennium. If the Y2K bug generates computer errors, the confident certainty in the complex calculations that lie at the heart of these derivative contracts would be destroyed. Moreover, the sheer size of the financial derivatives market could mean that its collapse could easily trigger the crash of the rest of the stock market.

Consider the following excerpt describing financial derivatives from a *TIME* magazine article published on April 11, 1994:

> Computer-generated, hyper-sophisticated financial instruments that use the public's massive bet on securities to create a parallel universe of side bets and speculative mutations so vast that the underlying $20 trillion involved is almost five times the total value of all stocks traded on the NYSE in a month and three times the size of the nation's GDP. . . . These breakneck derivative deals are possible because Wall Street today has transformed itself into a virtually seamless network of computer-linked brokers, dealers, and exchanges around the globe. The trades take place in an electronic never-never land that can be entered from anywhere in the world. . . . Billion dollar transactions involving derivatives or other securities that once took hours or days to handle are now routinely completed in seconds—with all the potential risk or reward that comes with instant gains and losses.[1]

The financial derivatives market has exploded. Over $22 trillion is at risk in America, and $45 trillion is at risk worldwide. To place these figures in perspective, the total value of all stocks traded on the New York Exchange amounts to only $6 trillion. We should remember that a large drop in the financial derivatives market precipitated the stock market crash in 1987, which resulted in the loss of almost $1 trillion of investors' funds. The largest Japanese steel company lost $1.3 billion in a derivatives trade a few years ago, while the largest steel company in Germany lost $1.4 billion. Orange County, California, lost $2 billion, and the 270-year-old Barings Bank of England was forced into bankruptcy by a 28-year-old trader who lost $1.3 billion on a derivatives contract in seven days.

The latest reports suggest that as much as $42 trillion is now at risk at any one time in the computer-driven financial derivatives markets. The substantial amount of money at risk in these extremely dangerous trades represents an amount that exceeds the total value of all the stocks and bonds in America by more than four times! This is almost unbelievable, but absolutely documented and true. Aside from the inherent risk of huge losses of billions of dollars to the investors, corporations, and the banks that are deeply involved in the world of financial derivatives, the Year 2000 computer crisis presents a new danger to these incredibly complex computer trades that may bring the entire financial community to its knees as we enter the new millennium.

The computer errors that are certain to infect the banks' and stock market's computer systems make it a near certainty that many financial derivative contracts will suffer from errors or loss of important data necessary to calculate and complete a trade. The failure of the financial derivatives markets, because of the size of the funds at risk, may quickly destroy the rest of the market. Clients who lose big on their derivative contracts will be forced to liquidate their stock and bond holdings. This action could certainly trigger the long feared bear market that will collapse the longest bull stock market in history.

Escape the Year 2000 Economic Collapse

Despite the 1929 financial disaster, those who were forewarned and got out of the market in time, survived the Great Depression, and recovered. During the depression of the 1930s, over ten thousand Americans became millionaires (the equivalent of $10 million in today's dollars). They saw the warning signs before the 1929 crash, preserved their cash, and got out of debt, stocks, and investment real estate before the collapse of prices. Those who prudently acted early were then in a position to acquire quality real estate, equities in solid companies, and other undervalued investments at a fraction of their previous price. Hopefully, we can learn from history and apply those lessons to the potential financial dangers we face as the year 2000 nears.

Notes

1. *TIME*, April 11, 1994.

8

The Military Y2K Crisis

The Danger of the Year 2000 Crisis to America's Military Defense

The United States military is the most powerful armed force in the world. It is able, on short notice, to bring significant military forces against any conceivable adversary. Due to constant downsizing of military manpower, the Department of Defense increasingly relies upon extremely sophisticated weapons systems. The United States military and intelligence community use more computers than the military forces of all other nations combined. Therefore, America is a military superpower, able to project its power anywhere across the globe in support of United States policy and its own national security concerns. However, its overwhelming dependence on computers may place the United States at an extreme disadvantage in the year 2000, when many of its weapons systems and communications systems are likely to fail.

The U.S. Department of Defense depends upon millions of computers, billions of lines of sophisticated computer code, and billions of embedded microchips. Initial estimates concluded that up to 358 million lines of computer code need to be checked and fixed. Many weapons, from night-vision telescopes to cruise missiles, depend totally on the accurate functioning of their computer components. Edward Yourdon, the author of *Time Bomb*

2000, calculates that the U.S. military has more computer software than the entire American business community. He estimates that it may have to check, fix, and test as many as 30 billion computer program instructions. It is highly unlikely that this will be accomplished in time. Yourdon has written in his book that "the Year 2000 work that the Department of Defense faces will be by far the largest and most difficult project it has ever undertaken. Frankly, we think the odds of it finishing all of its work on time are zero."[1] In confirmation of this pessimistic reading of the situation, Congressman Stephen Horn gives the Department of Defense a grade of C– in terms of its readiness to face the next century.

Professor Keith Bennett, head of the computer science department of Durham University in the United Kingdom warns, "Unless action is taken by the Ministry of Defense and the Pentagon we will inevitably see their entire computer systems shutting down; their computers could crash and there will be chaos."

Emmett Paige, the U.S. assistant secretary of defense in charge of command, communications, and intelligence, testified the following before a Congressional hearing on April 16, 1996:

> The impact of taking no action on the Year 2000 problem is that we risk the high probability of severely hampering, in some cases, many defense activities. Some of those activities will involve military operations. Does this place some of these operations at risk? I believe that it does. . . . The Department of Defense has some relatively unique Year 2000 problems. . . . Our software inventory includes software written in computer languages, such as JOVIAL, that are not widely used elsewhere. This is a legacy of past policies that permitted the proliferation of different computer languages and dialects. . . . This means we will need a wider array of software tools to help reduce the time to find and fix Year 2000 problems, and to validate the solutions through testing.

> Commercial off-the-shelf software tools are available only for some of the more commonly used computer programming languages, such as COBOL, C, and, of course, ADA. For many computer languages, no

commercial tools are available. . . . In the Department of Defense we are dramatically raising the awareness of the Year 2000 problem across the board, from the department's senior leadership to its systems personnel and its suppliers in the commercial sector. . . . We have set in motion a campaign to find and fix the problem in our weapons systems and automated business information systems. We are also working with other federal agencies and private industry to increase awareness and solve this ubiquitous problem.

In a recent report on the dangers of Y2K, John Hamre, the deputy secretary of defense, warned the U.S. Senate Armed Services Committee that the U.S. Defense Department had over 3,000 "mission-critical systems that may trigger a serious disruption if they failed to work." An additional 28,000 other computer systems need to be fixed throughout the nation's defense network. Remember that a single system out of the 3,000 mission-critical systems, might encompass something as broad as the F-18 fighter-bomber computer radar system, which includes thousands of planes that are vital for the nation's defense. The U.S. Defense Department has already spent several billion dollars on fixing the Y2K problem, but much more must be spent in the immediate future to assure that the military can provide adequate defense for the nation as we enter the next millennium.

One study concluded that the Department of Defense had over six million separate computer software applications, scattered in bases across the world, containing over 30 billion COBOL computer program instructions. At the present time, over 200,000 computer specialists are involved in maintaining the military's present computer systems. Because of downsizing during the last decade, there are no surplus computer programmers that can be assigned full time to the Y2K crisis. The U.S. military would need to hire over one hundred thousand additional COBOL-trained programmers in order to fix its most mission-critical programs before the January 1, 2000 deadline. Unfortunately, the history of past military computer software projects suggests that the Department of Defense has seldom completed deadlines like this on time, within budget, or completely. This will be the most expensive and difficult project ever faced by the Department of Defense. Most objective commentators have concluded that it is impossible for the military to fix all of their systems on time. Many critical military systems may enter the next millennium with potentially dangerous and expensive flaws.

As the U.S. Department of Defense has downsized its military forces in the last two decades, it has increasingly relied upon sophisticated computer systems to replace expensive soldiers to provide control over powerful advanced weapons systems. However, as the most computerized military force in the world today, the U.S. Department of Defense is extremely vulnerable to the dangers of corruption from the Year 2000 bug. Almost every one of the powerful weapons systems in the U.S. military—including our sophisticated attack bombers, our advanced fighter planes, our powerful Trident submarine force with super-accurate D5 multitargeted nuclear warheads, and our new Star Wars particle beam generators—are in some way dependent on accurate date calculations. The Department of Defense computer systems were built using hundreds of now-obsolete computer languages, such as JOVIAL, TACPOL, NELIAC, CS-1, and CMS-2, languages developed between the 1960s and the early 1980s. Unfortunately, the young computer specialists in the military poorly understand these obsolete computer languages. This unfamiliarity with the source code language makes finding the Y2K problems in the machine code almost impossible in the little time remaining before the deadline.

A U.S. General Accounting Office report entitled AIMD-97-149 deals with the readiness of the Department of Defense for the Year 2000. The report is extremely doubtful that the military can become Y2K-compliant on time.

> If CCSS (Commodity Command Standard System) cannot correctly process dates on and after January 1, 2000, military equipment such as tanks, artillery, aircraft, missiles, munitions, trucks, electronics, and other supporting materials for the soldier in all likelihood will not be ordered, stored, transported, issued, paid for, or maintained.

> Mobilization plans and contingencies would be significantly impaired if materiel were delayed. However, LSSC (Logistics System Support Command) has yet to

resolve several critical problems associated with the assessment phase to ensure that (1) systems are adequately tested, (2) contingency plans are developed, and (3) interface partners are fully aware of LSSC's Year 2000 plans. Furthermore, during the same time that LSSC is addressing the Year 2000 issue, the agency is also working to implement considerably more software projects than it has in the past. This unprecedented workload is compounded by a reduced staff level and LSSC's basic lack of a mature software development and maintenance process. Together, these factors raise the risk level of the Year 2000 project beyond what is normally expected of a software modification effort of this magnitude.

Until these problems are resolved, LSSC is not well positioned to move forward into the more time-consuming phases of renovation, validation, and implementation. As a result, we believe LSSC will find it increasingly difficult to prepare CCSS in time for the arrival of the year 2000.[2]

The U.S. Defense Department Will Share Data with Other Nuclear Powers

The Pentagon is now planning to share critical data with the world's other nuclear powers to avoid the danger of an accidental nuclear exchange caused by computer errors in the year 2000. Deputy Secretary of Defense John Hamre informed the Senate Armed Services Committee that the Defense Department does not believe that Y2K could actually trigger an accidental nuclear exchange. However, the military plans to minimize the possible risk of an accidental war by sharing sensitive data with Russia, Britain, France, China, etc., about the dangers of malfunctioning missile launch early-warning systems and nuclear attack warnings. The Year 2000 computer crisis for the military has now become a national security issue. Hamre said the U.S. Defense Department is going to establish a Year 2000 program with the major nuclear-armed countries to make certain that the Year 2000 won't make "the screens go blank" throughout the nation's military command and control headquarters.

John Hamre admitted that the U.S. Strategic Command, which oversees the United States' entire nuclear force composed of

ICBMs, stealth and B-52 bombers, and the fleet of Trident submarines with their powerful D5 missiles, is already holding "technical discussions" with the Russian military regarding Y2K problems. Lt. Gen. Kenneth Minihan is the director of the National Security Agency, America's top-secret intelligence agency, which breaks the secret codes of every nation on earth. Minihan recently warned the Senate that they are deeply concerned that most other nations do not realize the risks to their national security from the approaching Year 2000 crisis. "Our concern is that Russia and China have only a rudimentary understanding of the dangers that the Year 2000 might have on their nuclear command and control systems." Hamre noted that one of the challenges in fixing the Y2K problem in the Russian military is that much of the old Soviet computer programming code was usually written by individual programmers without proper documentation.

Although nothing has appeared in the media, I have received intelligence reports from private sources in the few weeks prior to this writing that a simulated Y2K test on four ICBM missiles in a Montana missile complex produced distressing results. After setting the clock to January 1, 2000, the failure of some of the hundreds of embedded microchips within the complex computers that control the fail-safe presidential missile control launch system caused catastrophic equipment failure. Two of the four missiles refused to launch during the simulated test. The other two missiles went into unauthorized launch mode and would have fired.

New Computerized Miniaturized Weapons

America's military research labs have been attempting to develop a new weapons system that potentially would leave our adversaries defenseless. A report in the *South China Morning Post* newspaper on February 28, 1998 (originating from *Agence France-Presse* in Hamburg, Germany) warned that America's defense industry may produce new, incredibly microscopic computer-controlled weapons. These weapons are so small they can be introduced unnoticed through door clefts, through vents in a computer casing, or into air-conditioning systems to attack soldiers or to disable strategic computer equipment. Unfortunately, these miniature weapon systems may also have Y2K problems, due to their dependence upon microchip time calculations.

Panorama magazine reported that a university in Tennessee designed an insect-sized mini robot. At the same time, a California research and development lab developed a miniature aircraft less than five inches long, designed for secret reconnaissance missions. Meanwhile, other California engineers have created robotic "microbats" that would attack enemy troops with miniaturized but lethal munitions. The Pentagon has also developed powerful microrockets that can penetrate enemy military command centers and cause short circuits that would disable sophisticated military computers. The reports indicated that the German Defense Ministry was taking these reports seriously and had requested that German military intelligence agencies investigate the "military possibilities of technical micro-systems."

The Threat of Information Warfare and Y2K

Recently the Center for Infrastructure Warfare Studies Assessment completed a study on enemies of the Western powers. They revealed the possibility that these enemies may use the vulnerability that Y2K will cause as an opportunity to attack the nation's military and intelligence computer systems. The primary security concern is that enemy nations, or independent groups of computer terrorists, may choose to launch "referenced attacks" that will lie dormant until the systems reboot their computers after a shut down (in response to Y2K problems). The second stage of this cyber-warfare attack may trigger the dormant virus to cause significant damage to the computer system before it can be detected. A number of military experts now believe that the next major attack against the United States of America will be launched through the Internet rather than through traditional means of conventional warfare. The vulnerability of all our computer systems to the Y2K bug has made major computer systems throughout the world vulnerable to sabotage.

Problems with the Global Positioning Satellite System

The Global Positioning Satellite (GPS) system was created by the U.S. Navy to guide its high-tech cruise missiles, troop carriers, planes, and advanced satellites to their precise locations. The system began working on January 5, 1980. Each satellite contains a computer and atomic clock that keeps precise time. After a few years, the navy decided to make some of this technology available to civilians. For the last twenty years, this GPS system has been immensely helpful to boaters and many other travelers. For example, tens of thousands of transport trucks have GPS receivers that enable a company to track the precise location of its trucks to determine if someone has stolen the cargo or whether the driver has simply deviated from his planned route. The GPS receivers perform complex calculations that measure the time it takes the signals to travel from the satellite, located twelve thousand miles away in space, to the user's location on earth. Measuring the exact time in microseconds that it takes the signals to reach that location (from two or three of the satellites) allows the microchip in the GPS receiver to triangulate the location to within a few yards.

The GPS navigational system is so accurate and easily accessible that over ten million of these devices have been sold over the last few years. These devices are used worldwide by mountain climbers, hunters, boaters, as well as by soldiers.

Unfortunately, the designers included a date glitch, similar to the Y2K millennium bug, within the internal calendar program that runs inside the twenty-eight U.S. satellites. The designers included a counter that keeps track of the number of weeks, up to a total of 1023 weeks, as well as the exact time. On August 21, 1999, the GPS clocks will calculate that the 1023rd week has finished and will automatically reset to zero. When that occurs, many older GPS receiver devices will miscalculate the user's position (as though it was January 5, 1980) and begin producing huge errors. Thinking that the date is January 5, 1980, some receivers will calculate that the satellite's radio signals have been travelling for 19 years and conclude that the user is billions of miles from the satellite. A climber in the Rocky Mountains may check his GPS receiver on August 22, 1999, and be surprised to learn that the receiver now thinks the climber is somewhere in Egypt or Jupiter.

All branches of the U.S. military are now frantically checking their ground receivers to be certain that the sets will still work properly next year. An air force spokesman has stated that the air force has verified that its GPS system will work properly. The problem is entirely with the microchips in the older GPS receivers, not the satellites. It is essential that civilian users of the Global Positioning System immediately get in touch with the manufacturers of their equipment by the summer of 1999 to assure it is compliant. Experts suggest that GPS receivers manufactured after 1996 are likely to work properly. However, older GPS receivers should be examined to see if they need new microchips. Many banks also use GPS receivers, connected to their computers, to provide superaccurate time calculations that enable the financial institutions to calculate interest payments. If the individual banks do not correct their own GPS receivers, they will inadvertently create interest miscalculations.

Inaccurate Department of Defense Compliance Reports

The latest reports from the military reveal that they are at least four months behind their schedule to fix their Y2K problems. The recent report by the Defense Department's inspector general stated that a number of information technology managers were producing positive reports, stating that their critical systems were Y2K-compliant, despite the fact that their systems were not tested, nor had they received Year 2000 certification.

The U.S. inspector general submitted a report on the military's Y2K efforts, and concluded, "Senior DOD management cannot afford to make Y2K program decisions based on highly inaccurate information. . . . If DOD does not take the action that it needs to obtain accurate information as to the status of its Y2K efforts, we believe that serious Y2K failures may occur in DOD mission-critical information technology systems." One of the most worrisome aspects of this investigation is that the inspector general found that "the existence of a completed and signed Y2K-compliance checklist did not always mean that the system was Y2K-compliant."

A word to the wise: Beware of companies or governments using the term "Year 2000 Certified." These words do not necessarily mean that the system will operate perfectly following January 1, 2000. Sally Brown, a U.S. Department of Defense official who is working with the military to solve this problem, warns, "The word certified had so many different kinds of meanings that it had lost all its meaning."

Notes

1. Yourdon, Edward and Jennifer Yourdon. *Time Bomb 2000.* Upper Saddle River: Prentice Hall, 1998.

2. "Defense Computers: LSSC Needs to Confront Significant Year 2000 Issues." GAO report AIMD-97-149, September 26, 1997. Found on the Internet at http://www.gao.gov/new.items/ai97149.pdf.

9

The Problem with the Government's Computers

To place the significance of the Year 2000 crisis in perspective, we need to consider the fact that over 33 percent of every dollar expended in the United States economy is spent by the American government at the federal, state, and local levels. If the government is unable to solve its Y2K problems by the deadline, the impact on the rest of society will be enormous. The rippling effect from its collapse will bring down a large part of the rest of the economy, inexorably tied to government activities.

The government faces much greater problems than most American corporations. The U.S. government's Office of Management and Budget submitted its quarterly report, entitled "Progress on Year 2000 Conversion." This report revealed that eighteen out of the twenty-five federal government agencies are planning to implement their Y2K solutions in the final three months of 1999. Despite the promises of solutions, the November 1997 report of the House Congressional Subcommittee on Government Management, Information and Technology had given eight federal government agencies a D report card regarding their actual readiness. According to the government's own sources, these agencies will not meet the January 1, 2000 deadline. If you hoped that these noncompliant agencies might not affect the life of the average citizen like yourself, consider the list of these agencies: the Department of Defense, the IRS, the Departments of Energy, Education, Agriculture, Health and Human Services, and Transportation. We are truly facing the worst crisis since the darkest days of World War II.

A recent report from the federal government reveals that the government's oversight agency, the Office of Management and Budget (OMB), has discovered that an incredible 8,589 vital and mission-critical federal governmental computer systems throughout the United States will not be Y2K modified. The OMB recently completed a study that determined that 13 percent of these computer systems cannot be fixed in time, and, therefore, must be completely replaced before January 1, 2000. They also concluded that 62 percent of the government's computer systems need to be analyzed, repaired, and tested before the deadline. Amazingly, despite the years of warnings in computer and technical articles since 1986, 98 percent of the 5,332 mission-critical systems were not repaired or adequately tested as of mid-1997. Apparently, some 12 percent of the government's critical computer systems have been repaired, but still must be tested to ascertain their compliance. Almost 85 percent of the most critical computer systems that run virtually every aspect of the government have not been fixed and tested, as of the spring of 1998. There are simply not enough computer programmers nor enough time or money to solve the majority of Year 2000 computer problems before the arrival of New Year's Eve, 1999. The majority of computer researchers now believe that most agencies of the U.S. federal government, including the Department of Defense, the IRS, and the Department of Health, will fail to solve their Y2K problems on time.

Republican Congressman Steven Horn is the Chairman of a House subcommittee that monitors the U.S. federal government's efforts to solve the Year 2000 computer crisis. Since 1997, Congressman Horn has been assessing the progress of the Executive Branch through his quarterly report card on the Y2K problem. Every quarter the government fails to meet the necessary standard required to solve the problem before the disaster hits.

On March 4th, 1998, Horn revealed in a press conference that the government agencies are simply failing to marshal the necessary resources in time to save their agencies from catastrophe. He said, "The executive branch is . . . on the edge of failure. [They have] almost 8,000 mission-critical computer systems. . . . At the current rate of progress, only 63 percent of these systems will be ready for the date change. . . . We have a long way to go and a short time to get there."

Chairman Horn responded to the administration's promises to fix the Year 2000 by saying, "This Subcommittee finds it very troubling that twelve of the fourteen federal departments plan to implement their solutions in the final three months of 1999. This strikes me as dangerously optimistic planning—especially since this Subcommittee has monitored dozens of government computer modernization programs that have seldom, if ever, been completed as planned on time and on budget."

When Congressman Horn considered the plans of various government agencies to solve the problem in time, he concluded that it was virtually impossible. In his report, Representative Horn described his evaluation of the government's claim that the majority of U.S. government agencies would only "implement their solutions in the final three months of 1999. Perhaps it is possible for thousands of computer programmers in hundreds of locations to rewrite millions of lines of code with the precision and delicacy of a finely choreographed ballet. But I find it hard to believe the ballerina will also kick a field goal in the final seconds of the last quarter."

On May 15, 1998, Representative Horn's subcommittee issued the following report, grading these government departments on their readiness to meet the next millennium.

Congressman Steven Horn's Report[1]

Grading the Government's Agencies	The Grade as of May 15, 1998
Social Security	A+
General Services Administration	A–
Federal Administration Management Agency	A–
Department of Commerce	B
NASA	B

Nuclear Regulatory Commission	B
Department of the Treasury	C
Department of Labor	C
Department of the Interior	C–
Department of Agriculture	D
Department of Defense	D
Department of Justice	D
Department of Education	D
Environmental Protection Agency	F
Department of State	F
Department of Health and Human Services	F
Department of Energy	F
Department of Transportation	F
Administration Overall	F

Hearings were recently held in the House of Representatives. Attorney Sally Katzen, President Clinton's close personal friend and top official in charge of the Y2K problem for the Office of Management and Budget (OMB), issued the following statement: "We have made a good start. While we . . . are concerned about the limited time we have left, and the large amount of work that remains to be done, we are confident that we will finish that work so that the year 2000 computer problem will be a non-event." Incredibly, despite ample warnings from computer consultants and admissions of the approaching disaster from many government departments, the government's spokesman declares that "the year 2000 computer problem will be a non-event."

One of the most knowledgeable government computer technology experts is Joel C. Willemssen, who works with the General Accounting Office (GAO). At the same hearing, Willemssen gave an entirely different analysis of the readiness of the government to meet the Year 2000 deadline. He contradicted the optimistic report that Sally Katzen's OMB had just issued. Willemssen declared, "OMB's perspective that agencies have made a good start and that no mission-critical systems were reported to be behind schedule would seem to imply that there is no cause for alarm. On the contrary, we believe ample evidence exists that OMB and key federal agencies need to heighten their levels of concern and move with more urgency."

In addition to Willemssen's cautionary comments, we need to remember that the OMB quarterly reports concentrate almost exclusively on the corrective work being done on the government's mainframe computers. These reports totally ignore the danger to government operations from noncompliant desktop computers and embedded microchips. While it is essential that these mainframe computers be fixed on time, it is also essential that the tens of thousands of desktop PCs in government offices, as well as the millions of embedded computer microchips, be corrected.

The General Accounting Office concluded, in one of its recent reports to Congress, that "because of the potential for serious government-wide disruption to critical functions and services from the upcoming change of century, the Year 2000 computing problem has been added to our list of high-risk issues." This is an understatement. We need to keep in mind the well-known fact that only 14 percent of major software projects are completed on time, perform as promised, and meet their proposed budgets.

On June 15, 1998, when I searched the U.S. government's Federal Emergency Management Agency's (FEMA) Internet Web site, there was not a single mention of the Year 2000 computer crisis. Despite the fact that FEMA is charged with preparing for a variety of national disasters (from hurricanes to earthquakes), they have not made the public aware of the approaching crisis. In fact, the government's Office of Management and Budget's final quarterly report for 1997 on the readiness of the various governmental agencies to handle the Y2K crisis states that FEMA is so far behind in its preparations that they will miss the January 1, 2000 deadline by at least half a year.

Four representatives of Congress recently begged President Clinton to use his office to call the nation to arms to solve the Year 2000 problem before the crisis caused massive disruption and chaos. Representatives Morella (R-MD), Horn (R-CA), Gordon (D-TN), and Maloney (D-NY) pleaded with President Clinton to sign an executive order directing all U.S. government agencies to make the Y2K crisis their highest priority. Additionally, they asked Clinton to appoint a major government official to become the Year 2000 "czar" for the United States. Their letters included this statement: "Congress alone . . . cannot solve the Year 2000 problem. To date, many federal agencies have not, in our estimation, taken all the necessary steps to avert the pending crisis." Unfortunately, instead of responding with a televised message to the nation about the need to make this a national priority, Clinton merely cited solving the Y2K problem as number five in a list of general goals to be accomplished in his White House Millennium Project, a project designed to prepare the United States for the twenty-first century. Hilary Clinton is heading up this project, while simultaneously solving other emergencies such as "extending our unique and vibrant cultural life" and "reviving the spirit of citizen service."

This abdication of leadership by the leaders of the major nations throughout the world is disconcerting. Obviously, they are afraid of being criticized for failing to act sooner to solve this monumental problem. In addition, these leaders are probably fearful that telling the public the truth about Y2K now might trigger an immediate run on the banks and a stock market collapse. In a later chapter, I will explore the possibility of a hidden political agenda leading to a one world government that may utilize the Y2K crisis as a pretext.

President Clinton's Public Comments on the Year 2000 Crisis

To date, President Clinton's only message to Americans regarding the greatest technological and economic problem ever faced by the United States and the nations of the world, is as follows:

> Now, as the millennium turns, as we have all seen from countless reports, so do the dates on our computers. Experts are concerned that many of our information systems will not differentiate between dates in the 20th and the 21st century. I want to assure the American people that the federal government, in cooperation with state and local government and the private sector, is taking steps to prevent any interruption in government services that rely on the proper functioning of federal computer systems. We can't have the American people looking to a new century and a new millennium with their computers—the very symbol of modernity and the modern age—holding

them back, and we're determined to see that it doesn't happen.

Obviously, this response falls far short of the necessary "call to arms" that this desperate situation requires if the nation is to be adequately prepared.

An Open Letter of Warning to President Clinton

Professor Leon Kappelman (University of North Texas) is Co-chairman of the Year 2000 Working Group of the Society for Information Management (SIM). The SIM is a group of 2,500 computer specialists who work in the Information Technology (IT) groups of the top corporations in America. Kappelman has written a book dealing with the Year 2000 computer crisis. He recently wrote an open letter to President Clinton, warning him about the overwhelming dangers from the fast-approaching Year 2000 crisis.

President William Clinton,

Time is of the essence so I will be brief. I humbly ask you to please declare a national and global state of emergency because of the year-2000 (or century-date computer-processing) problem. I base this request not on some precognition about the future but on empirical evidence of both the enormous risks posed by this problem and on the minuscule probability that we will be able to effectively mitigate all of these risks in the time remaining.

Would you declare a state of emergency if you were informed today that millions of meteors, ranging in size from the diameter of a baseball to that of the moon, were due to strike earth on January 1, 2000? Metaphorically that is the situation we face. And just as people who examine the heavens without the benefit of telescopes might deny the existence of such meteors, this would not reduce the risks posed by them.

Whether we like it or not, the world is now in such a state of emergency. Regrettably we are not behaving as such and thus precious time is wasting. Fighting the century-date computer-processing problem is much like a war effort. But not only do we have the problem itself to defeat, but also the enemies of limited time as well as other resources, compounded by the near invisibility of the problem to the naked eye. The near 100 percent increase in total federal Year-2000-project cost estimates over the past few months is evidence of how little of this problem can be seen at first glance. Your leadership is intensely needed Mr. President.

Take the Nuclear Regulatory Commission (NRC) for example: Although the NRC publicly acknowledges century-date-related computer processing risks that are profoundly threatening to human lives and the environment, they refuse to require or take any action. Instead they rely on the unsubstantiated claims of parties who apparently have not actually tested any of these systems either—kind of like looking for meteors with the aid of a bottomless paper cup—and on some peculiar and irrational hope that no human errors could possibly occur if embedded-microprocessor and/or computer-based process-control systems do fail. . . .

The time for denial is long past. It is time for triage directed at a clear and urgent focus on the most life-threatening and mission-critical systems. Real tests of these systems are needed, not wishful thinking. Please ask to see proof, not just promises that all is well. Priorities must be set in order to focus limited resources of time and skills on repairing those systems that can cause the most damage, disruption, or death.

Sacrifices will be necessary. This will require some tough decisions by political, government, business, and other leaders. All of the year-2000-problem meteors cannot be stopped in time; thus we must focus our efforts on those that pose the greatest risks. A state of emergency declared by you is critically needed. As well as some facilitation of information sharing among countries, industries, and economic sectors. Time is wasting! Please Mr. President, send the world a wake up call before it's too late.

Senator Patrick Moynihan's Letter to the President Regarding Y2K

Senator Patrick D. Moynihan (D-NY) sent a letter to President Bill Clinton on July 31, 1996. It was published in the official Congressional Record on August 11, 1996. The letter effectively conveys the senator's concerns about the approaching Year 2000 computer problem. As a reader of this book, you might consider copying this letter and giving it to someone who does not believe this Year 2000 problem is real. In light of the fact that this document is now in the public domain, you are free to create unlimited copies.

Senator Patrick Moynihan
U.S. Senate, Washington, D.C.

The President,   July 31, 1996
The White House,
Washington, D.C.

Dear Mr. President:

I hope this letter reaches you. I write to alert you to a problem which could have extreme negative economic consequences during your second term. The "Year 2000 Time Bomb." This has to do with the transition of computer programs from the 20th to the 21st century.

The main computer languages from the '50s and '60s such as COBOL, FORTRAN, and Assembler were designed to minimize consumption of computer memory by employing date fields providing for only six digits. The date of this letter in "computerese," for example, is 96-07-31. The century designation "19" is assumed. The problem is that many computer programs will read January 1, 2000 as January 1, 1900. Computer programs will not recognize the 21st century without a massive rewriting of computer codes.

I first learned of all this in February and requested a study by the Congressional Research Service. The study, just now completed, substantiates the worst fears of the doomsayers. (A copy of the CRS study is attached.) The Year 2000 problem ("Y2K") is worldwide. Each line of computer code needs to be analyzed and either passed on or be rewritten. The banking system is particularly vulnerable. A money center bank may have 500 million lines of code to be revised at a cost of $1 per line. That's a $500 million problem. (I learn from Lanny Davis that his client, the Mars Company, estimates the cost of becoming Y2K date compliant at $100 million to $200 million. Mars is only a candy company.) One would expect that a quick fix of the problem would have been found but it hasn't happened and the experts tell me it is not likely.

There are three issues. First, the cost of reviewing and rewriting codes for Federal and state governments which will range in the billions of dollars over the next three years. Second, the question of whether there is time enough to get the job done and, if not, what sort of triage we may need. I am particularly concerned about the IRS and Social Security in this respect. Third, the question of what happens to the economy if the problem is not resolved by mid-1999? Are corporations and consumers not likely to withhold spending decisions and possibly even withdraw all of their available funds from banks if they fear the economy is facing chaos?

I have a recommendation. A Presidential aide should be appointed to take responsibility for assuring that all Federal agencies including the military be Y2K date compliant by January 1, 1999 and that all commercial and industrial firms do business with the Federal government also be compliant by that date. I am advised that the Pentagon is further ahead on the curve here than any of the Federal agencies. You may wish to turn to the military to take command of dealing with the problem. The computer has been a blessing; if we don't act quickly, however, it could become the curse of the age.

Respectfully,

Senator Patrick Moynihan

The Commission for Critical Infrastructure Protection

President Clinton signed Executive Order 13010 in July 1996, which established a Presidential Commission for Critical Infrastructure Protection (PCCIP). While this order does not specifically mention the Year 2000 computer crisis, there is no question that this was one of the major concerns, as was the growing perception of dangers from attacks on our infrastructure through computer terrorism and technology-information warfare.

Executive Order 13010 reads as follows:

Certain national infrastructures are so vital that their incapacity or destruction would have a debilitating impact on the defense or economic security of the United States. These critical infrastructures include telecommunications, electrical power systems, gas and oil storage and transportation, banking and finance, transportation, water supply systems, emergency services, and continuity of government. Threats to these critical infrastructures fall into two categories: physical threats to tangible property and threats of electronic, radio-frequency, or computer-based attacks on the information or communications components that control critical infrastructures. Because many of these critical infrastructures are owned and operated by the private sector, it is essential that the government and private sector work together to develop a strategy for protecting them and assuring their continued operation. [italics added]

President Clinton established this extraordinary presidential commission in 1996 to deal with various "threats" to "national infrastructures," including "computer-based attacks on the information or communications components that control critical infrastructures." Executive Order 13010 totally ignored the man-made Year 2000 computer crisis.

Interestingly, the commission also published a Frequently Asked Question (FAQ) for Critical Infrastructure Protection. This FAQ answered one question about the Year 2000 computer crisis with the following response: "As a part of its overall research on the vulnerabilities of America's infrastructures, the Commission is taking a look at the problem that may arise from the inability of some computers and other automated systems to properly process dates beyond December 31, 1999."

On October 13, 1997, the PCCIP issued a 180-page report called "Critical Foundations." Mr. Tom Marsh, the chairman of the commission, wrote the following statement: "We found no evidence of an impending cyber attack which could have a debilitating effect on the nation's critical infrastructures. While we see no electronic disaster around the corner, this is no basis for complacency." This report all but ignores the millennium computer virus.

Finally, on February 4, 1998, President Clinton began to respond seriously to the Year 2000 Crisis. He signed an executive order commanding every agency of the U.S. government to make solving the Y2K threat their number-one computer software priority. After years of publicly ignoring the Y2K crisis, Clinton also has created a presidential commission to deal with the Y2K crisis. In his executive order, the president wrote, "Unless appropriate action is taken, this flaw, known as the 'Y2K problem,' can cause systems that support those functions to compute erroneously or simply not run." He ordered all agencies of the federal government to "co-operate with the private sector operators of critical national and local systems, including the banking and financial system, the telecommunications system, the public health system, the transportation system, and the electric power generation system, in addressing the Y2K problem."

While this order finally awakened every part of the vast American governmental machine to the impending crisis, it is simply too little, too late. The failure of governments in almost every nation to make Y2K a national emergency back in 1995 (when we would have had time to fix every system) will probably be recorded by future historians as the greatest example of ignorance, incompetence, and negligence in human history. All of us will endure the consequences.

People Are Already Jumping off the Year 2000 Ship

At the same time President Clinton finally issued a series of executive orders establishing emergency Y2K committees, the country's most talented people in charge of solving the computer crisis for many of the key infrastructure agencies of the federal government quickly decided to abandon their impressive careers and top salaries. According to the Information Technology Association of America (ITAA), in its February 6, 1998 report on the Y2K problem, the following people resigned their positions. The number-one person charged with leading the U.S. administration's efforts to solve the Year 2000 crisis, Sally Katzen, resigned in January 1998. Mr. Anthony Valletta, the top civilian official in the U.S. military dealing with the Y2K problem, was the acting secretary for command, control, communications, and intelligence for the Department of Defense until his recent resignation. The director for information management of the assistant secretary of defense and the information technology director also left their positions at the same time. Several days later, Arthur Gross, the head of computer technology at the Internal Revenue Service, also quit.

In the first week of February 1998, President Clinton created a special executive commission under a secret executive order to coordinate all government efforts to solve the Year 2000 problem and push all agencies to maximum effort. The United States finally acknowledged the crisis, and the most knowledgeable people in the U.S. government left their posts. That same week, the top executives of the U.S. Department of Defense charged with solving this huge problem resigned their positions. Why? What do they know that the vast majority of the population does not know? Do they know that the problem is now far beyond the stage where it can be solved on time? Did these people resign their positions when they realized that their best efforts would still not ensure a successful resolution?

The problems facing state and provincial governments are just as urgent and daunting. The comptroller for the state of New York, H. Carl McCall, made the following statement regarding New York's readiness: "Unless significant progress is made quickly to solve the state's Year 2000 Computer Problems, New York is facing a potential crisis in the delivery of government services. . . . Although time is running out, the state and local governments are just waking up to the extent of the challenge."

In 1997, the U.S. General Accounting Office (GAO), Congress's investigative agency, printed eight reports that explored the government's readiness for the Y2K deadline.

Significantly, all eight reports warn that the U.S. government is tragically unprepared for the full impact of the Y2K crisis. For example, the GAO report on the readiness of the Social Security Administration (SSA) declared, "While SSA deserves credit for its leadership, the agency remains at risk that not all of its mission-critical systems—those necessary to prevent the disruption of benefits—will be corrected before January 1, 2000."

Year 2000 Progress of Federal Departments and Agencies[2]

(Mission-Critical Computer Systems Only)

Government Department or Agency	Total # Systems	Done at Deadline	Not Done at Deadline	Estimated Completion
Social Security	308	100%	0%	1999
National Science Found.	21	100%	0%	1999
Veterans Administration	11	100%	0%	1999
Agriculture	1,319	100%	0%	1999
Commerce	470	100%	0%	1999
Environmental Prot. Agency	61	100%	0%	1999
Housing & Urban Dev.	63	100%	0%	1999
Off. of Pers. Management	124	100%	0%	1999
Small Business Admin.	40	100%	0%	1999
General Services Admin.	58	85%	15%	2000
Interior	95	88%	12%	2000
Justice	187	75%	25%	2000
Nuclear Regulatory Comm.	7	71%	29%	2000
Health and Human Svcs.	491	74%	26%	2001
NASA	158	73%	27%	2001
Treasury	327	60%	40%	2001
Agcy. for Int. Devel.	7	58%	42%	2001
Energy	370	66%	34%	2001
FEMA	48	77%	23%	2001
Education	14	63%	37%	2002
Transportation	617	33%	67%	2003
Labor	61	26%	74%	2007
Defense	2,915	36%	64%	2009
State Department	78	40%	60%	2014
Entire U.S. Government	7,850	63%	37%	No Date

A few cautions regarding this report: (1) It ignores 60,000 other government computer systems that are considered non mission critical systems. (2) It ignores the hundreds of millions of embedded computer chips used in government agencies. (3) It ignores the millions of government desktop computers and programs that will fail.

What Does the Government Say about Its Preparations for the Year 2000?

President Clinton appointed John Koskinen as the new Y2K "czar" in charge of getting the U.S. government on track. However, Koskinen's comments in an interview for the Year 2000 Law Report on April 1, 1998, are not very comforting. He said, "Both the President and the Vice President are very much engaged on this issue. In fact, this Administration has been focused on the Year 2000 Problem for several years. . . . I believe all critical federal services will continue without disruption on January 1, 2000." In light of the objective evidence presented in this book and in Congressman Horn's quarterly Readiness Reports, it is hard to understand on what basis the government can make their optimistic claims.

During Koskinen's testimony before several congressional subcommittee hearings in the spring of 1998, he made several comments that suggest that the government does not yet fully grasp the true enormity of the problem, such as, "As you know, the President shares your concern." If true, then why has the president not called the nation to meet this emergency? To date President Clinton has spoken less than 130 words publicly about the Year 2000 crisis. Another Koskinen remark: "Agencies are making progress but the rate of that progress needs to increase." Then why do all reports, including Rep. Horn's, reveal that agencies are falling steadily behind in their goals of fixing their critical systems on time?

Koskinen said, "The Council can play an important role in meeting those challenges." He spoke of the Council's role as "a catalyst . . . a facilitator . . . a coordinator." Tragically, these comments, and most of the reports on this problem by the government, treat the Y2K crisis as business as usual.

Mr. Koskinen told the committee members about a meeting

with the director of the Federal Emergency Management Agency (FEMA), the person who is in charge of foreseeing and responding to national disasters. The head of FEMA told Mr. Koskinen that his agency will "begin to work closely" with state and municipal disaster authorities in the near future, and will "offer whatever support they can." In Congressman Horn's Y2K Readiness Report (based on the government agencies own assessment of their ability to solve the problem by Jan. 1, 2000), FEMA admits that they will not have their computer systems Y2K-compliant until sometime in 2001. Consequently, it is difficult to place much faith in FEMA's promises to assist other government agencies in meeting the deadline.

The True State of the U.S. Government's Y2K Problems

Capers Jones, a brilliant software consultant who is considered the leading expert in the area of software metrics and cost analysis, has written many technical books. His book entitled *The Year 2000 Software Problem: Quantifying the Costs and Assessing the Consequences* is based on his years of detailed research. Recently, Jones made a speech in Washington, D.C., in which he shared a number of critical estimates regarding the government's readiness for the Y2K deadline:

- 58% of federal government Y2K projects are behind schedule
- 14,250 military applications will not be fixed by January 2000
- The total Y2K cost for the federal government will be at least $143 billion

Senator Moynihan was one of the first leaders in Congress to become concerned about the possible impact of Y2K on America. In the spring of 1996, the senator requested that a study be completed to determine the dangers. According to testimony recorded in the Congressional Record on August 11, 1996, the evidence presented proved that Senator Moynihan's fears were well founded: "Many managers initially doubted the seriousness of this problem." The U.S. Congressional Research Service, part of the Library of Congress, made a detailed study of the Year 2000 problem and the probable impact on government operations in response to the senator's request. The study concluded, "Due to a lack of time and resources, the majority of . . . government agencies will likely not fix all of their computer systems before the start of the new millennium."

What is the basic strategy of governments around the world in dealing with the Year 2000 crisis? Unfortunately, to date—as of the early months of 1998—most governments have followed a threefold strategy: (1) talk, talk, talk; (2) hold meetings and appoint management committees to discuss the problem endlessly; and (3) periodically announce that everything is fine and that they will solve the problem by the year 2000 (with no supporting evidence). In other words, "Trust us. Has your government ever lied to you before?" Some would reply, "Well, as a matter of fact, yes." The government's only number-one priority until January 1, 2000 seems to be to keep the population calm and avoid a panic that might lead to the worst run on the banks in history.

In congressional hearings about the Y2K problem, Senator Moynihan questioned Ms. Willis, a representative of the congressional General Accounting Office, about the dangers the Y2K problem posed to the normal functioning of the Internal Revenue Service (whose tax revenues are essential to the daily functioning of the U.S. government). This was the recorded exchange that followed:

Senator Moynihan: "What is your feeling about the IRS?"

Ms. Willis: ". . . The IRS is the largest civilian Year 2000 conversion in this country, possibly the world. . . . They are aware of the problem but they have a very long way to go and time is running out. . . . In a couple of weeks we will be in a better position to come back and give you a better assessment."

Senator Moynihan: "I hope you will because this could bring the whole system crashing down."

Ms. Willis: "It could be catastrophic."

The Internal Revenue Service

Arthur Gross, assistant IRS commissioner and key spokesman of the Internal Revenue Service (IRS), released the following statement: "The best estimate now is the IRS has to plow through forty million lines of computer code and 30,000 applications." In a later statement, Arthur Gross called the IRS's Year 2000 conversion task "massive" and described a project that will examine and correct more than a hundred million lines of code and almost 50,000 applications.

While it is natural for many Americans to feel little sympathy for the less-than-beloved Internal Revenue Service, a few minutes of sober reflection will reveal that a breakdown of the computer systems of the government's tax collection agency would cause hardship to every citizen in the country. If the government cannot collect over a trillion dollars in taxes, custom duties, etc., then it will be unable to pay its millions of civilian and military employees. How long would government computer programmers stay on the job trying to fix the IRS computers if they were not paid?

Knowledgeable computer programmers suggest that the IRS computer system is hopelessly complicated and that many of its major computers are unable to communicate with each other. During the last eight years, the IRS management has spent one billion dollars in an unsuccessful attempt to solve its "Tower of Babel" computer chaos. The U.S. Congress became so exasperated at the agency's demonstrated failure to fix its computers that it cut off all funding for the project. They felt that the money was being thrown into a black hole. To make a desperate situation even more hopeless, Congress added more than eight hundred pages of complex tax-code changes during the last few years that needed to be programmed into the IRS's computers. Add to these problems the fact that the Y2K crisis presents an inflexible deadline that cannot be delayed or evaded. Most observers believe that major parts of the IRS will not be able to fix their computers on time. In a statement made at a recent Washington conference, Arthur Gross said, "Failure to achieve compliance with Year 2000 will jeopardize our way of living on this planet for some time to come."

An article in *The Los Angeles Times* (Oct. 16, 1996) reported on the IRS problems: "The [agency] is launching a massive effort to forestall a breakdown of the income tax system when 2000 arrives. . . . If the agency cannot quickly revise millions of lines of obscure software code, . . . [the problem] will throw the government's financial operations into chaos. Computers throughout government and private industry face the same problem." The article went on to report that the federal government "has been dangerously late in recognizing the [magnitude of the] problem." Recent reports suggest that the IRS has more than 100 million lines of computer code that must be carefully examined, corrected or replaced, and then tested for bugs before we can have any confidence that their problems are fixed.

The inability of the IRS to correctly audit a taxpayer's tax-return compliance may encourage some taxpayers to underreport income, claim spurious deductions, or fail to pay taxes at all, in the hope that the computer confusion will make it impossible for the IRS to catch them. In a voluntary tax-filing system such as exists in America and Canada, the vast majority of taxpayers file their tax forms and pay their taxes correctly. They know that, ultimately, the tax authorities can track their sources of income and expenses with sophisticated computer systems. However, the approaching crisis in 2000 will certainly adversely affect the government's ability to collect the tax revenue that is essential for the nation to function.

To make matters worse, there are reliable indications that the IRS is not the only tax agency with huge computer problems. One of the most knowledgeable experts on the Year 2000 problem is Dr. Gary North, author of *The Remnant Review*. He has an excellent Web site on the Internet (http://garynorth.com) that compiles the latest information from government and industry on the state of the crisis. Dr. North reported in April 1998 that, to date, "no government tax collection agency above the county level is Year 2000 compliant today."

A Possible IRS Collapse

At a U.S. House Ways and Means Committee hearing on the Y2K problem on May 7, 1998, the Commissioner of the IRS testified about the potential disaster America faces in its tax collection efforts in the year 2000. The commissioner warned Congress that it would not be possible for the IRS to incorporate these hundreds of tax-code changes authorized by Congress in 1997 and fix its Y2K problems at the same time. The commissioner warned that unless Congress postponed the tax-code changes, it would be "virtually impossible for the IRS to ensure that its computer systems are Year

2000 compliant on January 1, 2000, and would create a genuine risk of a catastrophic failure of the nation's tax collection system in the Year 2000."

This admission by the top IRS official revealed that, basically, the situation is out of control; they have run out of time. Some members of Congress are so convinced that the IRS is going to fail in 2000 that they are attempting to build political support for a contingency tax bill that will establish a flat tax system (17 to 20 percent) in the year 2000. In light of the probable failure of the IRS to operate correctly in the opening months of the year 2000, it would be wise to carefully consider your income tax deductions to avoid creating a situation in which the IRS owes you a tax refund. If the IRS commissioner's own dire predictions come true, you could be waiting for that tax refund for a long, long time.

In Canada, Revenue Canada has indicated that they are confident that they will have their tax-collection computer systems Y2K-compliant in 1999. Furthermore, the Canadian human resources department that handles old-age pensions and unemployment insurance checks appears to be doing well in their program to correct their Y2K problems. However, no one will give an absolute guarantee that these essential governmental systems will function properly.

The Department of Treasury

The Department of Treasury has the second largest number of computers and software code next to the Department of Defense. Congressman Stephen Horn's December 11, 1997 Y2K score card revealed that the Treasury Department was so far behind that they will not be able to repair even their most critical computer systems until 2004. As late as May 7, 1998 the General Accounting Office's specialist on Y2K, Joel Willemssen, admitted to Congress that they had not even begun to actually repair any of their code yet. So far they were still assessing the extent of the problem. When you consider that the Treasury controls the nation's money supply, the IRS, Treasury Bills, and government bonds you can see that a major catastrophe is possible that may trigger staggering economic consequences.

Economists have calculated that there is only enough paper and coin currency to provide approximately $1000 in actual cash for every American citizen. However, the fact that American currency has become the world's reserve currency has resulted in over half of all U.S. currency being held offshore by foreigners in other nations. Therefore, less than $500 cash is actually available for every citizen. When the banking runs begin sometime in 1999 the available currency will vanish very quickly. Those who have the foresight to acquire some cash early will be in a much better position to deal with the crisis during the first few months of the year 2000 until major systems are restored and running normally again.

The Possible Collapse of Welfare and the Social Security System

On one hand, the U.S. Social Security Administration (SSA) is the most prepared of all government agencies to cope with the January 1, 2000 deadline because they began to seriously address the problem years ago (in 1989). In fact, they claim in their published report (Feb. 15, 1998) to Congressman Stephen Horn's House Subcommittee on Government Management, Information and Technology that they have already fixed or will fix by 1999 nearly all of their 308 mission-critical computer systems that are responsible for generating over 51 million Social Security checks every month.

However, even if the Social Security Administration fixes its computers, that will not mean that Americans can sleep peacefully; their pension checks are still not safe. It turns out, on close inspection of the Social Security setup, that this government agency does not actually make direct payments of its obligations to the tens of millions of older citizens. Each month, after preparing a complete list of citizens that qualify to receive their monthly pension check, the SSA sends the list electronically to an agency called the Financial Management Service (FMS), which is part of the U.S. Treasury Department. The Financial Management Service is the agency that actually sends out the checks or makes the direct deposits to each pensioner's bank account.

On April 1, 1998, the Year 2000 Law Report reported on Treasury Secretary Robert Rubin's testimony to a House of Representatives subcommittee about the treasury's Year 2000 problems: The only bureau left with truly serious Year 2000 issues is Financial Management Service. That bureau, which handles a wide range of financial transactions for almost every government agency—including the administration of the Electronic Federal Tax Payment System—continues to be the area we're most concerned about. Unfortunately, the entire Social Security Administration may totally fail in its mission to American citizens if it cannot send out the millions of checks, through the Financial Management Agency, that Americans expect to receive in their mailbox each month.

This situation illustrates a problem that will affect every government agency, corporation, and ministry in the world. Even if time and money is allocated to solve the internal Year 2000 problems, companies or agencies are still remarkably vulnerable to the hidden problems that stem from the unsolved Y2K computer problems of suppliers, bankers, and customers. The ultimate problem of the Year 2000 computer crisis is that all governments, corporations, charities, and individuals are so intricately interconnected by millions of hidden computer systems that a breakdown in one system will almost certainly infect the many other systems whose managers thought they were safe. Unless every single business or government agency tests their Year 2000 corrected system with every one of their interconnected suppliers, customers, and government agencies, they will never be able to confidently assert that they are absolutely ready for the year 2000.

An article in the *Jerusalem Post* on June 13, 1997 reported that "when January 1, 2000, arrives, Israelis could wake up to find that their national insurance benefits are not arriving, their income tax file is nowhere to be found, and their education records indicate they never completed the first grade. The 20th century may have augured in the technology age, but a small glitch in the system may wreak havoc when the new millennium arrives. Known alternately as the Millennium 2000 Problem, the Millennium Bug, or YK2, the glitch reflects a shortcut computer programmers took in order to save byte space." The article warned that "unable to move ahead to the next century, confused computerized weapons systems could lose track of their missiles, stock markets could crash, and airplanes could get lost in mid-flight, as air traffic systems fail." Jim Sinur, the vice president of research for the Gartner Group, warns, "The alarm bell has rung."

Where Does the Government Spend Its Money?

Consider where the U.S. government spends the enormous tax revenues that it acquires from American taxpayers, and you will soon appreciate the immediate and devastating implications if the IRS and other tax-collection agencies' computers fail to handle the Year 2000 computer crisis correctly. According to the authoritative American governmental *Statistical Abstract of the United States*, the expenditures of the government can be broken down in the following areas:

- 22 percent goes toward Social Security
- 17 percent is directed to education, technology, transportation, etc.
- 16 percent of American taxes goes toward defense
- 15 percent of the budget goes toward paying the interest on the national debt
- 11 percent pays for Medicare medical costs
- 19 percent pays for a variety of entitlement programs (pensions, etc.)

The U.S. government acquires from its taxpayers, and pays out through the above agencies, over \$1 trillion every year. However, as a result of the approaching Year 2000 computer crisis, those \$1 trillion may be paid out in error or disappear into cyberspace because of the government's failure to correctly solve this problem in time.

The State of Y2K Readiness of Various Nations

While the Y2K crisis affects every single nation on earth, the level of awareness and readiness to face the computer problems varies greatly from nation to nation. The Gartner Group is probably the most experienced and respected consulting company in the world that is dealing with the Year 2000 computer crisis. Their consultants are working closely with governments and businesses in dozens of nations throughout the world. Because of their close association with hundreds of corporations and government agencies in numerous countries, they have a very accurate understanding of the actual state of compliance within the various nations across the globe. The four key sectors that will profoundly affect every citizens' life are the Y2K impact upon government taxation and pensions as well as the vital areas of banking and electrical power.

Canada, Australia and New Zealand

According to the reports from Gartner Group and other consultants, Canada, Australia, and New Zealand are among the leading nations in fixing both their governments' computer systems as well as the systems used by their business communities. Fortunately for Canada, Peter de Jager, one of the leading Y2K consultants, has been warning both the government and corporations since 1993 that this is a very serious problem. Peter de Jager wrote an important article on this crisis in the September 6, 1993 issue of *Computer World* magazine. Unfortunately, most of his colleagues dismissed his warnings as being extreme. After years of warnings, Canada's government and its major corporations began working on Y2K in 1995 or 1996. An edict went out from the prime minister's office in 1996 that no other software programming projects were to be completed until the various governmental agencies had first solved their Y2K problems. The federal government's Treasury Board Secretariat has overseen the various departments' compliance. The Year 2000 problem is addressed as a monthly issue at every meeting of government administrators. Unfortunately, the evidence from recent reports suggests that the ten provincial governments are not nearly as well prepared for the approaching deadline. For example, on June 17, 1998, auditor Erik Peters warned the provincial government of Ontario that many of its departments are not on target to fix their Y2K problems before the deadline. It is distressing to realize that many municipalities and cities across the nation are almost oblivious of the danger to their computers from this problem and have barely begun to address it.

Another factor that helped Canada in dealing with this crisis is the fact that as a huge country with a relatively small population, it has a tradition of strong monopolies in both industry and commerce. This situation resulted in only five major banks providing most financial services throughout the nation. The benefit is that these five huge banks were able to provide the funds and corporate commitment to work together on the Year 2000 computer crisis. Consequently, with both the essential federal governmental functions of taxation and pensions, as well as the normal operation of its banks likely assured, Canada will at least have a strong infrastructure as it begins the Year 2000. The situation in Australia and New Zealand parallels the situation in Canada. However, provincial and municipal governments and the majority of businesses are likely to suffer severe Y2K disruptions.

The United States of America

Although the general awareness of the Y2K problem has been very minimal until the summer of 1998, U.S. federal, state, and local governments had begun working on their computer systems in 1997 and early 1998. Unfortunately, for many complex systems this will prove to be too late. The vast majority of U.S. government agencies claim they will fix their computer systems in the final months of the year 1999, leaving almost no time for detailed testing. In light of the well-established precedent of government officials exaggerating their ability to meet a given deadline, it would be wise to treat all promises of compliance with considerable reserve. Knowledgeable observers expect major and costly failures of computer systems and a crippling of the ability of the government to provide normal services during the initial months of the next millennium. The vulnerability of the banking system to Y2K is multiplied by the fact that America has 9,500 banks.

Russia, Eastern Europe, Asia, Africa, and South America

The news from these areas of the world is not hopeful. In many cases, these regions are totally ignorant of the Y2K problem and believe that it will not affect them. When the United Nations asked 180 nations to verify their computer's readiness to handle the millennium bug, only 37 nations responded that they were even aware of the approaching danger. One Arab nation in the Middle East reported that it had not seen the "millennium bug yet, but when it appeared, they planned to spray it."

In Asia, Russia, and the Third World, government officials and corporations are largely unaware of the danger.

Consequently, financial centers such as New York and London are already planning on cutting off electronic computer communication with these nations to prevent them from crashing American computer systems. Surprisingly, despite the obvious sophistication of the Japanese economy, there is a staggering lack of awareness of the problem or plans to deal with the necessary computer modifications in the time remaining. Up to 70 percent of Japanese corporate software has been created in-house and customized. Unfortunately, this makes it impossible to solve this problem by purchasing a new upgraded software package from a commercial vendor. Each custom software program must be laboriously examined and fixed on its own.

Notes

1. *USA Today*, June 8, 1998.
2. This data was prepared for Chairman Horn and his House Subcommittee on Government Management, Information, and Technology on February 15, 1998.

10

The Impact of Y2K on Business

The largest manufacturer in the world is General Motors. The tens of thousands of computers that control its automobile production lines, track deliveries, monitor invoices, etc., contain two billion lines of computer code. Using the very conservative industry estimate of one dollar to check and correct each line of code, the enormous Y2K programming project will cost General Motors more than $2 billion. Vice President Ralph J. Szygenda, General Motors' chief information officer, admitted in an interview, "The Year 2000 problem is serious and costly and won't go away. This is not going to be quick, and its not going to be easy."

One of the top industry experts dealing with the Year 2000 problem is Larry Martin, the president of Data Dimensions, a major company that has been helping corporations resolve their Year 2000 programming problems since the early 1990s. Larry Martin was asked to give his testimony on the general level of Y2K preparedness to a U.S. Senate committee that was examining this issue. Martin stated, "Current estimates by reliable industry groups suggest that only one-third of U.S. companies and government agencies have seriously started work on a Year 2000 fix. And the rest of the world has been even slower to take action. . . . We would roughly estimate that only 5 percent of the total work to complete Year 2000 compliance has been accomplished." In follow-up comments, Martin also warned of the danger to business that exists if the banks fail to fix their own Year 2000 problems. "The lack of concern and action on the part of the international banking community is particularly distressing. The ability of international banks to operate effectively after the Year 2000 is, in our estimate, seriously in question."

Another situation that will cause problems for many businesses is the license restrictions associated with almost all of their computer software applications that corporations have purchased. If the original software manufacturer fails to make the software Y2K-compliant or to provide a new upgrade, the business will naturally be forced to ask its own programmers to modify the software. However, that decision will have two unfortunate legal consequences. First, the modification of software usually violates the software license and exposes the business to the risk of a lawsuit for infringement of the intellectual copyright owned by the company that created the original software. Second, a business's modification of the software will usually result in the legal violation of the warranty; therefore, the business will not be able to sue the software manufacturer for failure to make the software Y2K-compliant.

The Devastation Caused By Year 2000 Computer Problems

Capers Jones is one of the most respected computer consultants in the world. He has studied the Y2K problem extensively and published a study called *The Economic Impact of the Year 2000 Computer Software Problem.* Jones has concluded that the impact on Western industries will be severe, resulting in major job loss and many bankruptcies.

In his report, Jones makes the following assessment of the impact from the Year 2000 crisis:

- Up to 1 percent of the largest corporations in America and Canada will go bankrupt, causing massive loan failures and employment losses. These companies individually employ tens of thousands of employees.
- Another 5 to 7 percent of mid-size North American

corporations will fail, resulting in banking losses and major layoffs. This means that up to 2,000 corporations will likely fail, resulting in the layoffs of up to 10,000 employees each (20 million possible layoffs).

- An estimated 3 percent of very small corporations (employing an average of 100 employees) will be destroyed by Y2K—a potential of up to 180,000 of these firms, untold billions of dollars of investment, and the elimination of as many as 18 million jobs.

Recent reports on the Internet from the well-respected investigative firm Kroll and Associates reveal that the New York Mafia has entered the Y2K business by setting up consulting corporations that infiltrate corporations, with the intention of diverting millions of dollars to mob bank accounts (without the knowledge of the client). An article in the *New York Post* by Beth Piskora also warns of the sophisticated mob plans to steal tens of millions of dollars from unsuspecting corporations.

The Surrender Strategy: A Y2K Disaster in the Making

After procrastinating and denying the dangers of the Y2K problem for years, a significant number of computer department managers have decided to surrender. Interviews with computer specialists suggest that some information technology managers have already concluded that they cannot possibly complete the needed repairs for their company's or agency's computers before the January 1, 2000 deadline. Consequently, some managers have decided to take a sabbatical in the fall of 1999 and possibly return in the spring of 2000 to assist the companies that have survived the computer holocaust.

Some companies, after considering the overwhelming costs and time constraints, have simply decided that it is more feasible to sell their company to a competitor who has already fixed their systems than to attempt to struggle through the year 2000 with their present noncompliant computers. Other corporations have decided either to shut down or merge with larger corporations rather than spend hundreds of millions of dollars.

Small Business

Across North America there are six million small businesses which may suffer serious disruptions or total business failure if their Y2K problems are not corrected in time. These small businesses are the real engine of our North American economy. The vast majority of new jobs, inventions, and technological developments come from these millions of small businesses that are the true entrepreneurs in our nation. However, a survey by the National Federation of Independent Business reveals that the vast majority of these businesses are either unaware, unconcerned, or financially unable to deal with the Y2K problem. Many of them are hoping that the government or Bill Gates of Microsoft will somehow fix their computers before the deadline is reached. Unfortunately, the likelihood of finding a universal "silver bullet" solution to fix all vulnerable computer systems is between slim and none. The problems are simply too complex with hundreds of different computer systems, over 500 different computer languages, billions of lines of computer code, and billions of embedded microchips. While 75 percent of small businesses declared that they knew about the Year 2000 computer crisis they have taken no practical action to avoid the dangers. Incredibly, over 50 percent of these small companies admitted that they have no plans to fix their systems before January 1, 2000.

A senior researcher at the NFIB Education Foundation, William Dennis, calculated that up to 330,000 small businesses are in serious danger of bankruptcy unless they fix their systems and another 370,000 may be forced to close their offices and production plants for a period of time during the first few months of the year 2000 because of huge computer errors. Those who remain unconcerned about the dangers of Y2K to our economy should consider the fact that small businesses, which are essential to our prosperity and full employment, are the least able to technically or financially respond to this overwhelming challenge.

Will the Year 2000 Crisis Cause a Recession?

The Year 2000 Group (Washington, D.C.), sponsored by the Fannie Mae Corporation, recently published a survey on the conclusions of their group's membership, which consists of corporate and government executives concerned with the Y2K issues. More than 65 percent of the respondents think that the Y2K crisis will cause America and the global economy to suffer an economic recession. More than 50 percent of the group expects a mild recession, and more than 35 percent expects a strong recession, causing social unrest. Over 10 percent of those surveyed concluded that the millennium virus will trigger a full-scale economic depression.

Many business experts believe that Y2K will result in the loss of profitability of many corporations and the bankruptcy of many other small corporations and mid-size businesses. This would trigger significant increases in unemployment. Alan Greenspan, chairman of the U.S. Federal Reserve, has publicly predicted that there is a 40 percent risk of a serious recession.

Mr. Graeme Inchley, the head of the Australian government's Year 2000 initiative, has also predicted that the computer crisis will collapse many small companies and possibly trigger an economic recession. Mr. Inchley gave an interview in which he said, "The Government is going through an assessment of its areas of greatest risk and will have to move very quickly in order to at least be able to operate by 2000. . . . There will be areas of Government that will not be year 2000 compliant and we need to be prepared to put work arounds in place. This is a very serious problem indeed." He also focused on the dangers from noncompliant personal computer systems: "There are about 10 million PCs in Australia and if only 5 per cent of them fail to operate on January 1, 2000, then we will have a major problem."

In warning of the dangers of an economic recession occurring early in the Year 2000, Inchley noted, "It only takes 10 percent of Australia's small businesses to fold at one time to bring on a recession. There is a strong possibility that the figure will be much greater than 10 percent because of the failure of small business to act. We're not just talking recession but major economic meltdown." Mr. Inchley concurs with the assessment of Dr. Edward Yardeni, the chief economist of Deutsche Morgan Grenfell, that the risk of a Y2K-led global recession now exceeds 60 percent.

Y2K and European Business

The situation regarding businesses in Europe is very disturbing. Despite years of warnings, the vast majority of European corporations are not making significant progress in solving their Year 2000 problems. According to a study conducted by SRI International, almost 74 percent of the companies in Germany report that they do not expect to complete their Y2K modifications before December 31, 1999. While a number of major firms (such as Siemens and BMW) claim they have fixed their Y2K problems on time, the majority of small to mid-size European firms are unprepared to face the dangers of their noncompliant computer systems on January 1, 2000. In Germany and in the rest of Europe, there is still no evidence of a strong demand that every government and corporation make the Year 2000 problem a national priority, comparable to preparation for war, so that everyone would be forced to take action.

Another well-respected computer consultant, Peter de Jager, has expressed grave concern about the ability of the European nations to complete their massive euro currency computer conversion project during the same time frame that they must make their computers Y2K-compliant. Either project by itself represents the greatest computer software conversion project in history. To expect tens of thousands of corporations and government agencies in Europe to simultaneously complete both projects is to ask programmers to do the impossible. Peter de Jager has compared the demand for Europe's computer programmers to repair their computer systems to accommodate both the euro currency conversion and the Y2K conversion at the same time to requesting them to "run the four-minute mile with a bathtub strapped on our backs." In other words, Europe has almost no chance of making their computer systems Y2K-compliant because they must devote all of their energies and talents to get their systems ready to handle the new euro currency properly.

Obviously, the greatest challenge to businesses anywhere in the world will be the possible loss of electrical power for a few days or more if the utilities have severe computer problems. If the Nuclear Regulatory Commission shuts down nuclear power plants for safety reasons, many states and provinces will experience serious power shortages for some period of time.

Brownouts and occasional blackouts are possible, depending on your location. Businesses in Europe, Asia, South America, and Africa, where work on Y2K problems has only just begun, may suffer from longer power outages.

The Y2K Liability Nightmare

Many law firms are having their partners attend seminars to learn of ways to sue companies that produce errors because of Y2K problems. Unfortunately, for those who are sued, defending against such lawsuits will be difficult because it will be hard to argue successfully that the problem was unforeseen. Articles about this problem have appeared in many trade magazines and mainstream publications over the last decade. Some experts, including the Gartner Group, estimate that the amount of money that will be involved in Year 2000 lawsuits will exceed $1 trillion. Many corporations will be forced into bankruptcy by lawsuits, causing large financial losses and the unemployment of many people. Many directors and executives of organizations that are negatively impacted by Y2K problems may find themselves sued by unhappy shareholders who suffer losses, angry workers who are laid off for months, and customers who lose the supplies necessary for their own company's survival. Unfortunately, insurance policies will not likely provide coverage because the Y2K problem was not "unforeseen." It will be difficult to defend against such lawsuits. Private legal sources have informed me that one New York law firm has already settled more than 200 lawsuits "out of court," for an average settlement exceeding one million dollars as of June, 1998.

11

A Cashless Society

Preparations for the Mark of the Beast

In the book of Revelation, the prophet John prophesied the creation of a cashless society in the last days. He foretold that the possession of the number "666" as proof of your allegiance to a future world dictator would be essential to enable anyone to "buy or sell" in that future society. This was an incomprehensible prophecy when John proclaimed it two thousand years ago. However, recent technological events now make it possible to replace paper currency and coins with an electronic form of cash.

> And he causeth all, both small and great, rich and poor, free and bond, to receive a mark in their right hand, or in their foreheads: And that no man might buy or sell, save he that had the mark, or the name of the beast, or the number of his name. Here is wisdom. Let him that hath understanding count the number of the beast: for it is the number of a man; and his number is six hundred threescore and six. (Revelation 13:16-18)

As we approach the final months of this century, we are already 95 percent cashless in North America and in most of Europe. Less than 5 percent of the total money in our national economy actually exists as paper currency or coins. Several nations, including Finland, are quickly moving into the true cashless society. Canadians have embraced the new cashless society to such a degree that they now use as many debit card transactions per year as the United States, even though Canada's population is only one-tenth that of the U.S. The book of Revelation prophesies that the number 666 will be placed in a mark beneath the skin on the right hand or forehead to control people during the final three and a half years of the Antichrist's rule before the return of Jesus Christ. For the first time in history, engineers have developed technology that will allow tiny computer chips that contain your complete identification, medical, and financial records to be placed beneath the skin of the right hand or forehead.

Recently, scientists developed a miniature computer microchip so powerful that it can hold up to five gigabytes of information on a chip the size of a large grain of rice. Five gigabytes is as much information as what is contained in thirty complete sets of the *Encyclopedia Britannica*. This chip could easily be configured in a shape that could be injected beneath the skin. *Business Week* magazine reported that MasterCard International is testing a "smart card" computer chip that includes information about your fingerprint and identity that can be embedded in a credit/debit card. Card scanners in stores and banks will scan your fingerprint or voiceprint and compare it to the information on the card to verify your identity.[1]

Throughout history, man has used countless physical objects (including shells and cattle) as currency. Thousands of different types of money, composed of metals such as gold, silver, bronze, and copper, have been used by past societies. How could the apostle John have known about our new cashless technology unless God inspired him to write the words recorded in Revelation 13:16-18?

The New Smart Cards: The Coming Cashless Society

Technology is developing at such a rapid rate that we may all soon carry a single ID smart card, containing a computer chip, that will allow us to make phone calls, unlock our houses and cars, and buy anything from newspapers to televisions. MasterCard International is introducing a major campaign to promote the use of these smart credit cards by its 22,000 affiliated banks and the 12 million retail merchants that participate in their system worldwide. One of their motives is to reduce the spiraling losses due to credit card fraud (that now amount to over $500 million a year).

A November 1994 article in *Popular Science*[2] reported that college students are already using MCI's campus smart card system. MCI authorizes colleges to issue students a single smart card that will simultaneously serve as their photo ID, dorm room key, credit/debit card, and bank automatic teller card. In this system, a student can use a smart card to register for classes, take out library books, pay for cafeteria meals, and even pay for tuition. It is called the Campus Connections Card. It looks like a standard credit card, with the addition of a digitized photo of the owner. However, it contains two special magnetic stripes—one that allows point-of-sale transactions, the other for debit transactions. Florida State University was the first university to extensively use the system, but MCI is planning to introduce their system nationwide through a large number of colleges. Obviously, these multiple-use smart cards are just the beginning of a process that will culminate in every citizen using one single computer smart card to replace the variety of credit/debit and identification cards most of us now carry. The final step will be the replacement of the smart card with a tiny computer chip placed beneath the skin, which will provide a tamper-proof identification and financial authorization system to replace cash forever. One of my confidential sources, who works with VISA headquarters, has revealed that they are studying a new credit system that will actually use a miniature computer chip embedded beneath the skin instead of the standard credit/debit card to eliminate the possibility of theft, counterfeiting, or fraud.

One of the new technologies in the smart card field is called a "stored-value card," which acts as an electronic wallet. These stored-value smart cards contain a tiny computer chip that electronically stores a preset amount of money (such as $200) that you can use to purchase anything you want. You are able to purchase items by offering the cashier this card. The merchant will run the card through the reader and deduct the amount of that purchase, leaving the remaining balance to use to purchase other items.

An article in the *New York Times*[3] reported that stores and banks are strongly in favor of this new stored-value card system because it will eliminate cash transactions, which are expensive to handle and subject to theft. Increasingly, telephone companies are selling prepaid stored-value telephone calling cards that allow the purchaser to pay for long distance calls on public phones. A recent study shows that 90 percent of all cash purchases made each year by American consumers involve less than twenty dollars. In light of this fact, the advantages of stored-value cards are obvious. Electronic Payment Services, the bank-owned company that runs the MAC cash machines, is building a nationwide electronic smart card system.

A few years ago, this technology cost ten dollars per card, making them economically unviable. However, smart cards can now be produced for less than a dollar. One plan for their use would allow a customer to call his bank by phone, verify his identification by inserting the smart card into a slot in his special home phone, and electronically transfer funds from his bank account to his smart card. Many banks in Europe and Asia support the introduction of this new system. Several large banks in Britain are introducing a sophisticated Mondex smart card that stores money in up to five European or North American currencies and allows travel across Europe without worrying about carrying local currencies. Over 220 million smart cards are already in use across the European Union. By mid-1998, Mondex cards are expected to be used by merchants in Canada. The introduction of the Mondex stored-value card in America is imminent.

One of the latest inventions is the introduction of a form of electronic currency that can be used by consumers on the Internet, linking tens of thousands of interconnected computers and millions of consumers on the information highway. A European firm has created DigiCash, which can be purchased from a participating bank and then used electronically to purchase goods or services from other Internet patrons or companies. The firm's plan is to make the electronic currency anonymous. It would, theoretically, be untraceable, but a merchant could verify that it was a legitimate credit issued by a recognized bank, although the bank would be unable to identify the purchaser under this proposed system.

These technologies are being introduced by banks and governments throughout the world as preliminary steps on the road to the cashless society of the New World Order prophesied about in the Bible. Prophets foretold that money would cease to exist in the last days and be replaced by a cashless society that will use numbers instead of currency to allow you "to buy and sell." We are now rapidly approaching the moment when these ancient Bible prophecies can be fulfilled for the first time in history.

On June 17, 1998, a survey published on the Internet, by *CIO* magazine (a magazine for chief information officers) examined the awareness of average citizens to the Year 2000 computer crisis. The survey revealed that 62 percent of the people interviewed were aware of the millennium bug. However, an astonishing 38 percent of the respondents had never heard of the problem. The survey's most surprising statistic—and the one that should be most troubling to the nation's banking system—is the response to the question about what they would do if the banking industry failed to solve their Y2K problems by mid-1999. It is fascinating to note that 52 percent of the respondents said that they would move their money out of a risky investment or deposit. However, more than 25 percent claimed they would withdraw all of their money from the banks and keep it at home until the crisis was solved.

As noted earlier, less than 5 percent of the total money in the economy exists as paper currency and coins. If even 5 to 10 percent of customers attempted to withdraw a significant portion of their savings at some point in 1999, the banking system will collapse.

If that were to happen, it is probable that government officials and the banking industry would argue persuasively that the time has come to completely replace cash with electronic currency. This would avoid any future banking run because there would be no cash left in the banks. The technology does exist to replace cash with an implanted microchip. If this eventually happens, the stage will be set for the fulfillment of the Bible's ancient prophecy, described in the book of Revelation.

Notes

1. *Business Week,* June 3, 1996, p. 123.
2. *Popular Science,* November 1994.
3. *New York Times,* September 6, 1994.

12

A Secret Agenda for World Government

The elite groups who are attempting to create the New World Order and global government in the next millennium realize that the vast majority of the world's population is content with the existing situation of individual nation states. Polling organizations confirm that although citizens are happy to see the United Nations coordinating global peace-keeping and extending international assistance in the event of famines and other disasters, they are unwilling to transfer the sovereign powers of their nation to a new world government. The primary obstacle to world government is that most people love their local democracy, their country, their flag, their history, and their individuality.

Those people dedicated to creating a New World Order realize that the only practical way to achieve their goal is to create an economic, political, or military crisis of such vast proportions that no nation, on its own, could possibly solve it. The Y2K computer crisis provides a unique opportunity to impose a global government solution. Given the genuine potential dangers caused by the failure of the world's computer systems, citizens will be open to the practical solution of a world Year 2000 czar, who would have wide-ranging powers to find, fix, and test the world's computers to make sure society will be able to continue to operate properly in the next millennium.

The Need for a World Crisis to Further Globalist Plans

David Rockefeller, one of the key leaders of the Council on Foreign Relations, as well as the Trilateral Commission and the Bilderberger Group (organizations that develop strategies to create a global government), gave a speech outlining the global agenda and a preferred course of action to motivate world citizens to accept the concept of global government. In that speech he said, "We are on the verge of a global transformation. All we need is the right major crisis and the nations will accept the New World Order."

Plans to Elevate Gorbachev as the Global Year 2000 Czar

Recently, a conference on the government's response to the Year 2000 computer crisis was held in Washington, D.C., featuring Robert Bemer as the keynote speaker. The conference was called Drastic Measures For Drastic Times: Government Agency Assessment Testing, Conversion, and Best Practices for Year 2000 Compliance. Robert Bemer is well known in the computer world as the creator of ASCII code (a code that allows different computers to exchange text files, the concept of computer time-sharing, the COBOL computer language, and many other inventions critical to the world of computers). He has called for the U.S. government to create an all-powerful Year 2000 computer czar who would force every nation in the world to make the Y2K problem, and its correction, the number-one national priority.

In his speech, Bemer advised, "We must have national direction! I can say this with total sincerity, while still believing in minimal government. . . . So is there another Churchill in view? Someone has to be in direct and sole charge, without any other assignments to worry about. The name I have heard is Mikhail Gorbachev. Sounds good to me. He doesn't owe us much, and can't be bribed." Bemer continued, "If we can have a summit on global warming (which seems suspect, anyway), we should certainly have a global summit on the Year 2000 problem. If such could be mounted, it would ease the way to get someone of Mr.

Gorbachev's standing to be czar. What is the United Nation's position on this? Have they even discussed it?"

Mikhail Gorbachev, the former communist leader of the USSR, has now become the prominent spokesman of the Russian government's new Y2K awareness program. Incredibly, Gorbachev was the only official witness to testify before Representative Stephen Horn's Congressional House Information and Technology Subcommittee hearings on the Y2K issue on October 17, 1997. The global elite may be. preparing Mikhail Gorbachev to become one of the key leaders of the coming global government.

America and the Coming World Government

Some people ask how America could ever relinquish her sovereignty and join the coming world government in light of the safeguards provided by the U.S. Constitution. However, Congress has given the president powerful executive powers to enable him to seize total control of the U.S. government, the military forces, and the economy in the event of a national emergency. It is obviously essential that the president have legal authority to direct and control the resources of the nation to protect its citizens if America is ever attacked with nuclear weapons. A full-scale nuclear attack by Russia or China would therefore wipe out the military's command and control system and disrupt much of the normal functioning of government in America. It would be vital that the surviving political leadership of the United States retain the ability to control the government and military of America.

The range of almost dictatorial powers available to a U.S. president after he declares a national emergency equals the vast legal powers held by Adolf Hitler during his dictatorship in Germany. The existing emergency legislation allows a president to suspend the Constitution and exercise emergency powers whenever he determines that the nation faces a national emergency. However, the term "national emergency" is not defined by the law. It is left solely to the president to determine what constitutes a national emergency. Consequently, these executive orders are a loaded gun that a future president could use to establish a dictatorship and facilitate America joining a world government. An emergency could be declared at any time in the future and be used to enact legislation that Congress would never pass in normal times. The Year 2000 computer crisis will obviously create such an enormous economic and infrastructure crisis that the president would have ample justification to declare a national emergency and impose martial law.

The Presidential Executive Orders

These are some of the existing national security executive orders that a president could legally exercise during a declared national emergency.

- 10995: The seizure of all print and electronic communications media in the United States
- 10997: The seizure of all electric power, fuels, and minerals, public and private
- 10998: The seizure of food supplies and resources, public and private, including farms and equipment
- 10999: The seizure of all means of transportation, including cars, trucks or any other vehicles, including control over highways, harbors, and waterways
- 11000: The seizure of all American people for work forces under federal supervision (allowing the government to split up families if they believe it necessary)
- 11001: The seizure of all health, education, and welfare facilities—public and private
- 11002: The registration of every citizen by the postmaster general for government service
- 11003: The seizure of all airports and aircraft
- 11004: The seizure of all housing and finance authorities; authority to establish forced relocation designated areas that must be abandoned as "unsafe"; the establishment of new locations for population groups; the building of new housing on public land
- 11005: The seizure of all railroads, inland waterways, and storage warehouses, public and private
- 11051: The authorization of the Office of Emergency Planning to put the above orders into effect in times of increased international tension or financial crisis

In 1969, President Richard Nixon signed Executive Order 11490, which basically allows the president to suspend the

Constitution and replace it with martial law and a legal dictatorship during a national emergency. Conservative writer Howard Ruff commented on the dangers to freedom and democracy that exist in the establishment of these extra-constitutional powers: "Executive Order 11490 is real, and only the lack of a crisis big enough, a president willing enough, and a public aroused enough to permit it to be invoked, separates us from a possible dictatorship, brought about under current law, waiting to be implemented in the event of circumstances which can be construed as a national emergency."[1] The Y2K crisis could certainly constitute a national emergency and present a reason for the president to invoke at least some of the powers conferred on him by this series of executive orders. American freedom could be seriously imperiled as millions of computers across the country begin to fail, following midnight on New Year's Day, 2000.

Another executive order (Executive Order EQ 11921), signed by President Gerald Ford, ordered the Federal Emergency Preparedness Agency (FEPA) to plan for the establishment of total governmental control of the production and distribution of energy, wages, salaries, credit, and currency flow from all American financial institutions during a future national emergency. This order gives the president control of the nation. Furthermore, the order declares that during the duration of the emergency, Congress cannot reassert political control nor even review the matter for *six months*. In 1977, President Jimmy Carter replaced FEPA with the expanded Federal Emergency Management Agency (FEMA) which expanded these emergency powers.

Y2K: A Pretext for Emergency Laws and the Coming World Government

As mentioned in an earlier chapter, in July 1996 President Clinton signed Executive Order 13010, establishing a Presidential Commission for Critical Infrastructure Protection (PCCIP). This commission deals with the growing danger of attacks on our infrastructure through computer terrorism, computer information warfare, or the Year 2000 crisis. Executive Order 13010 refers to the threat to "critical infrastructures ... telecommunications, electrical power systems, gas and oil storage and transportation, banking and finance, transportation, water supply systems, emergency services, and continuity of government." The wording of the executive order specifically describes "computer-based attacks on the information or communications components that control critical infrastructures." Then, on February 6, 1998, President Clinton created a special executive commission under a secret executive order to coordinate all U.S. government agency efforts to solve the Year 2000 problem. Unfortunately, by this time, it was too late to be certain of fixing all of the mission-critical systems before the January 1, 2000 deadline arrives.

In light of the approaching danger of a complete economic collapse and a communications emergency caused by the Year 2000 computer bug, it is quite possible that the president of the United States, as well as the leaders of other nations throughout the world, will use existing national emergency legislation to take control of the banks and many other aspects of the national economy. Every Western democracy has comparable laws established to provide for the continuity of government in the event of a nuclear war or other national emergency. In Canada and the United Kingdom, these laws, called Orders in Council, were passed secretly by the Privy Council under the authority of the prime minister.

Under the McCarran Act, the U.S. president can legally suspend the Constitution and Bill of Rights, and with a single phone call impose martial law throughout the nation. Several reliable sources suggest that several U.S. government agencies have accumulated the names of millions of "suspect" American citizens. These citizens, whose names are maintained in a database in a high-speed Univac computer in Washington, are possible targets for arrest during a future time of national emergency. Some sources have suggested that these lists contain the names of prominent Christians and other patriots who have publicly expressed concerns about the move toward the New World Order.

The Plans to Recreate the Roman Empire

The ancient prophets of the Bible foretold the revival of the ancient Roman Empire in the final generation, when the Messiah would return to establish His eternal Kingdom. The prophet Daniel and the apostle John in his book of Revelation both foretold the rise of a European and Mediterranean super-state in the last days.

> And the fourth kingdom shall be strong as iron: forasmuch as iron breaketh in pieces and subdueth all things: and as iron that breaketh all these, shall it break in pieces and bruise. And whereas thou sawest the feet and toes, part of potter's clay, and part of iron, the kingdom shall be divided; but there shall be in it of the strength of the iron, forasmuch as thou sawest the iron mixed with miry clay. And as the toes of the feet were part of iron, and part of clay, so the kingdom shall be partly strong, and partly broken. And whereas thou sawest iron mixed with miry clay, they shall mingle themselves with the seed of men: but they shall not cleave one to another, even as iron is not mixed with clay. And in the days of these kings shall the God of heaven set up a kingdom, which shall never be destroyed: and the kingdom shall not be left to other people, but it shall break in pieces and consume all these kingdoms, and it shall stand for ever. (Daniel 2:40-44)

The Roman Empire began as a small city-state but rapidly rose to conquer the entire Italian peninsula in the third century before Christ. The Roman legions quickly conquered Carthage, in northern Africa, and most of the Greek empire in the centuries before Christ. Nations and city-states were crushed and overtaken by the well-disciplined and brutal legions of Rome. By the time of Christ, Caesar Augustus ruled most of the known world from Britain to the deserts of Syria. During the following centuries, the Romans expanded their empire to include present-day Romania, Bulgaria, Hungary, and Bosnia. Roman ensigns flew over the northern nations of Europe (including the territories of England, Switzerland, France, and Belgium) by A.D. 58, as the early Christian church began to send its missionaries across Europe and Asia. No other empire has ever ruled so vast a territory for such an extensive period of time. The iron kingdom of Rome lasted almost a thousand years. Unlike other empires that often absorbed and adopted the cultures and traditions of its conquered peoples, Rome crushed every nation beneath the feet of its deadly legions, destroying the existing culture and replacing it with the iron law and customs of Rome.

The language, culture, laws, and forms of government of the nations of Europe and North America are derived from ancient Rome. Although an entire millennium has passed since the end of Rome's imperial power, the prophet Daniel foretold that the Roman Empire would miraculously revive in the unique form of a powerful ten-nation confederated super-state in the last days. This was confirmed by the apostle John's prophecy (Revelation 13 and 17).

In the years following the devastation of World Wars I and II, the leaders of Europe held several conferences to plan a future federated European super-state. Their plan was to create a United States of Europe that would bring the major nations of western Europe together in a powerful alliance for the first time since the fall of the Roman Empire. In 1957, six European nations signed the Treaty of Rome and laid the foundation for the future United States of Europe: Italy, Germany, France, Belgium, the Netherlands, and Luxembourg. In the 1970s, the United Kingdom, Denmark, and Ireland joined the group. A ten-nation confederacy was created when Greece joined the group in 1979. In 1986, Spain and Portugal brought the total to twelve nations, the most powerful confederation of economic, political, and potential military power on earth. Now, the group has grown to include fifteen nations, as the Scandinavian nations and Austria have joined the European Union. Today, while the European Union includes fifteen nations, it may soon grow to include more than twenty-five, as negotiations are continuing with Turkey, Cyprus, Slovenia, Poland, and Hungary.

A BBC documentary on the European Union recently interviewed Belgian Foreign Minister Henri Spaak, the former secretary-general of NATO. Spaak admitted, "We felt like Romans on that day. . . . We were consciously re-creating the Roman Empire once more." The Maastricht Treaty has consolidated the current fifteen nations of the European Union into the world's first true super-state. The European Union is an economic, political, and potential military colossus that will soon dominate world events.

Toward a Ten-Nation Super-State

Chancellor Kohl of Germany has spoken publicly of a plan to unite five of the most committed nations of the European Union, who will surrender their sovereignty to achieve this super-state. This European superpower will possess an economy and population greater than America's. It will have one common army, a united economy, a single euro currency, and one political agenda. The plan anticipates that the ten remaining European Union nations will ultimately follow, and surrender their autonomy in future years as they consolidate their economies with the major states in the European Union.

The movement toward a three-tier system has already begun. France's Prime Minister Edouard Balladur discussed his vision of a three-tier Europe on August 30, 1994. The inner core of this new European Union will be nations "committed to full monetary, military and social union." The Germans have openly called for the creation of such a multi-tiered super-state structure in their document *Reflections on European Policy*. Germany and France argue for the creation of an inner circle of fully integrated European member states. Germany, France, Belgium, the Netherlands, and Luxembourg already form an inner ring of five key states. Britain, Italy, and Spain are part of the second group, a second ring of nations that wish to benefit economically but still retain some of their sovereignty. The third outermost ring of nations—Denmark, Greece, Portugal, and Ireland—desire the economic benefits but also without surrendering any of their sovereignty.

The prophets of the Bible described the revival of the ancient Roman Empire that would occur in the final years preceding the return of Jesus Christ. These prophecies indicate that the nations of Europe and the Mediterranean will voluntarily unite into a ten-nation confederacy that will ultimately become the political power base of a brilliant dictator, whom the Bible calls the Antichrist. Beginning with the ten nations of a united Europe, this man will use peace treaties and war to unite all of the nations on earth into one global empire.

A Global Government

The prophets Daniel and John warned that a global world government would rise in the last days and would be led by the Antichrist, the world's last dictator. John warned, "And it was given unto him to make war with the saints, and to overcome them: and power was given him over all kindreds, and tongues, and nations. And all that dwell upon the earth shall worship him, whose names are not written in the book of life of the Lamb slain from the foundation of the world" (Revelation 13:7-8). The prophecies by John and Daniel reveal that the whole population of the planet—"all that dwell upon the earth"—will be under the control of this global government, led by the Antichrist, in the last days. A single man, this future Antichrist, will have power "over all kindreds, and tongues, and nations" for the first time. There has never been a true world government during thousands of years of history. The increasing power of the United Nations, the International Monetary Fund, the World Trade Organization, and the World Court are rapidly destroying traditional national sovereignty and replacing national political motivations with a global economic agenda.

The elite who are committed to the concept of a global government have embarked on a program to subvert and diminish the traditional sovereignty of nation-states, including America and Canada. Henry Morgenthau, a former treasury secretary for President Roosevelt and a member of the Council on Foreign Relations (CFR), declared, "We can hardly expect the nation-state to make itself superfluous, at least not overnight. Rather, what we must aim for is recognition in the minds of all responsible statesmen that they are really nothing more than caretakers of a bankrupt international machine which will have to be transformed slowly into a new one." Morgenthau acknowledged that the key ingredient to this formula is their plan to "financially bankrupt the international machine." This is an astonishing admission of the global elite's willingness to manipulate the economic levers to produce an emergency situation that will allow them to impose new draconian laws that will move America toward global government.

Nations such as South Korea and Indonesia have accepted billions of dollars of loans from the World Bank and the

International Monetary Fund, and in doing so they have also accepted the tremendous political and economic price tag that comes with it. The price turns out to include the national sovereignty of these nations. The history of the last decade reveals that bailouts from the International Monetary Fund and the World Bank ultimately lead to a loss of sovereignty and independence by those nations that accept their loans during economic crisis. Nations such as Mexico, during its recent Peso Crisis, have been forced to turn to the International Monetary Fund (IMF) and World Bank for a financial bailout, but their leaders soon discovered that the stringent IMF loan conditions required that the borrowers abandon their national economic sovereignty to the control of the IMF bank advisors, who now attend every cabinet meeting and dictate terms. It is sobering to realize that these two UN institutions, the IMF and World Bank, are the very institutions that have the power to trigger a worldwide financial collapse that would allow them to seize control of these nation's economies. Furthermore, the actions and statements of their leaders revealed that they are clearly working toward the creation of a global government and a world-coordinated economy.

Two former UN officials, Sir Brian Urqhart and Erskine Childers, have written a provocative United Nations study called *Renewing the United Nations System.* This remarkable 1994 study was funded by the Ford Foundation, an institution known for its strong support of global government. The study recommended large-scale changes to streamline UN operations, including a recommendation that the United Nations General Assembly, the Security Council, the International Monetary Fund, the World Health Organization, and the International Labor Organization should be transferred into one central location to centralize political control while also improving overall efficiency.

This far-reaching United Nations proposal is clearly intended to set the stage for a future global government. Consider one quote from this study: "While there is no question, at present, of the transformation of the UN system into a supranational authority, the organization is in a transitional phase, basically shaped and constrained by national sovereignty, but sometimes acting outside and beyond it." Notice the phrase, "at present." This UN study repeatedly used terms such as "gradual limitation of sovereignty," "notable abridgements of national sovereignty," "chipping away at the edges of traditional sovereignty," and "small steps towards an eventual trans-sovereign society." These plans to progressively erode every nation's cherished sovereignty are discussed in every chapter of this extensive UN document, but nowhere is there a request or suggestion for a fundamental debate on these issues by the citizens and democratic representatives of each nation—no suggestion to debate the most sweeping political changes in history, changes that would allow major decisions, for more than 180 nations, to be made by unelected experts, behind locked doors, in completely undemocratic ways. The give-and-take of local and national democracy, which allows citizens to respond to the actions of its representatives, would be all but eliminated in any of the proposed global government scenarios. And yet, the suggestion of public discussion and debate is never raised.

The political leaders who are planning for world government realize that there is little public support for abandoning a nation's sovereignty in favor of global government. Therefore, the authors of this report recommend that the transition toward world government proceed stealthily step by step to avoid awakening a political backlash by the citizens of the Western democracies. Many of these recommendations in the UN report are very significant steps toward world government. The authors warn that the interim steps toward their goal must be taken very carefully "until the world is ready for world government."

Toward United Nations Global Taxation

The authors of the report argue that the United Nations should move toward financial autonomy by raising their own independent budget, financed through assessing a global surcharge tax on "all arms sales" and on "all trans-national movement of currencies." Other proposals suggest levies upon "all international trade, the production of such specific materials as petroleum," or alternatively, "a United Nations levy on international air and sea travel." Other recommendations in the UN report suggest an assessment of a "one day" income tax on every person on the earth once every year. This proposal to have the United Nations apply a global tax to every citizen on the planet is just one more indication of the United Nation's gradual transformation from an international consultative body to an emerging one-world super-state. This United Nations group has now suggested that the global tax also could be used to reduce government deficits and stimulate economic activity. *Renewing the United Nations System* lays out the required steps to bring about a powerful new world parliament on nations. This proposal of a global parliament is one of the key steps of the elite plan to build a consensus of widespread public support. The present UN system, since its creation in 1945, is an assembly of appointed representatives of mostly democratic national governments who negotiate and attempt to solve the world's economic, political, and military conflicts. However, there is an enormous difference between the existing structure of the UN and the newly proposed plan in which the UN parliamentarians would be directly elected by every citizen around the planet.

Will such a system of direct elections of global UN representatives provide true democratic input? The history of the directly elected European Parliament indicates that this idea is not promising. The European Parliament does not possess the fundamental democratic powers to directly choose the executives, to vote for laws, or to establish taxes. The real power in the European Union remains in the hands of the twenty-one-member appointed Executive Commission. The directly elected European Parliament is little more that a debating society, with very little real power or substantive influence, when compared to the powerful, appointed, but unelected European Union Executive Commission. The history of international institutions in this century shows that power is exercised by the members of the elite from behind locked boardroom doors. Their secret decisions are sold to the public through slick public relations and mass-media manipulation. The history of the last two thousand years strongly suggests that real democracy can only function practically at the local or national level. Once we move to the arena of international politics between nation-states, true democratic government is replaced by sophisticated tradeoffs negotiated behind the scenes. The European Union is a preview of where the true power will lie in the new world government.

The historian Arnold Toynbee, who strongly supported world

government, argued for global organization. "We are approaching the point at which the only effective scale for operations of any importance will be the global scale. The local states ought to be deprived of their sovereignty and subordinated to the sovereignty of a global world government. I think the world state will still need an armed police [and the] world government will have to command sufficient force to be able to impose peace. . . . The people of each local sovereign state will have to renounce their state's sovereignty and subordinate it to the paramount sovereignty of a literal world government. . . . I want to see a world government established."[2] Toynbee's words are no longer revolutionary. His rejection of the nation state is now shared by the financial and political elite who are planning to create a new world government.

In a *TIME* magazine article (July 20, 1992) entitled "The Birth of the Global Nation," Strobe Talbott, appointed by his friend President Clinton as deputy secretary of state at the State Department, argued that the nation-state is obsolete. He wrote, "All countries are basically social arrangements. . . . No matter how permanent and even sacred they may seem at any one time, in fact they are all artificial and temporary. . . . Perhaps national sovereignty wasn't such a great idea after all. . . . But it has taken the events in our own wondrous and terrible century to clinch the case." It is sobering to realize that some of the most powerful people in North America are working behind the scenes to produce a world government, regardless of the constitution or the desires of millions of North Americans for democratic and nationally elected governments.

The Club of Rome

In 1968, Aurelio Peccei founded and became president of the Club of Rome (COR) as a think tank to develop proposals for world government in order to further the globalist agenda. The Club of Rome is one of the most successful propaganda operations in this century. Significantly, the COR has suggested the need for a massive economic revolution that would transfer wealth from those who produce it to those in need. "Only a revolution, the substitution of a new world economic order can save us." The COR would like us to believe that the only hope for the survival of mankind is to surrender our rights, freedoms, and sovereignty to achieve world government.

Peccei openly calls for a world dictator, "A charismatic leader—scientific, political, or religious—would be the world's only salvation from the social and economic upheavals that threaten to destroy civilization. Such a leader would have to override national and international interests as well as political and economic structures in order to lead humanity away from the maladies that afflict it. . . . Only a revolution, the substitution of a new world economic order can save us."

The Ten Regions of the New World Government

As Aurelio Peccei describes in his fascinating book *Mankind at the Turning Point*, the COR "world model, based on new developments of the multi-level hierarchical systems theory, divides the world into ten interdependent and mutually interacting regions of political economic or environmental coherence." Peccei proposes that these ten regions of the world should consolidate into a one-world government by the year 2000.

- Region 1: Canada and the United States of America
- Region 2: European Union and Northwestern Europe
- Region 3: Japan
- Region 4: Australia, New Zealand, South Africa, Israel, and Pacific Islands
- Region 5: Eastern Europe
- Region 6: Latin America—Mexico, Central and South America
- Region 7: North Africa and the Middle East (Moslems)
- Region 8: Central Africa
- Region 9: South and Southeast Asia
- Region 10: Central Asia

Some have suggested that these ten proposed regions might be the fulfillment of Daniel's prophecy of the "ten toes" or the "ten horns" of the fourth world empire, the revived Roman Empire. However, a careful examination of Daniel's prophecy reveals that these "ten toes" and "ten horns" must refer to ten nations that will occupy the future territory of the historical Roman Empire. The Scriptures clearly indicate that ancient Rome will arise in the last days as a ten-nation confederacy within the Europe-Mediterranean area. The prophet describes this confederated union as being initially weak because it is composed of several strong nations ("toes of iron") and weaker nations ("toes of clay"). In Daniel's vision, the "eleventh horn," the Antichrist, will arise at some point in time after the ten nations unite as a confederacy. Then the Antichrist will violently "rip up three" of "the horns," representing three of these nations, and impose his satanic will on the rest of the ten-nation confederacy. Then the revived Roman Empire, led by the Antichrist, will become the most destructive empire in history, crushing everyone in its path.

The Powers of the United Nations Are Expanding

During an interview Douglas Hurd, the former British foreign secretary, stated that the United Nations must prepare to assume an "imperial role." Hurd declared that the United Nations must eliminate the traditional sovereignty of nations in order to assume military and political control when a nation such as Somalia or Cambodia collapses. During an interview at UN headquarters, Secretary Hurd said that we have entered "a new phase in the world's history." He warned that the UN must be able to intervene as early as possible to "prevent things from getting to the stage where countries are run by corrupt war lords, as in Somalia."

Many statesmen are encouraging a new form of neo-colonialism to replace the genocidal and corrupt regimes in several nations in Africa (such as Rwanda and Somalia). Some diplomats are proposing that the United Nations establish a "trusteeship" over nations that are hopelessly involved in famine or civil war, such as Bosnia. These tragic situations are ready-made for those who have an underlying goal to establish the United Nations as the nucleus of the coming world government.

Building a Global Security Force

Elite groups are planning to create a permanent standing army, a global security force that is powerful enough to allow the UN Security Council to impose the will of the world against any nation who dares to oppose its agenda. The United Nations has engaged in more peacekeeping operations in the last decade than it did in its first five decades.

The leaders of the United Nations have called repeatedly for the creation of a special UN rapid-deployment military force of sufficient size to defeat any potential opponent. The United Nations wants member states to provide trained soldiers, equipment, and necessary funding on a permanent basis, supported by each member-state's defense budget. The creation of a permanent United Nations armed force will be one of the milestones on the road to world government.

The worldwide Y2K economic crisis caused by the simultaneous failure of millions of computers and hundreds of millions of faulty embedded microchips may be the final crisis that will encourage the nations of the world to surrender. The need to establish global standards of computer communications, a possible worldwide common currency, and a new banking system may eliminate whatever remaining obstacles that stand in the way of the global government the Bible prophesies will rise in the last days.

Notes

1. Ruff, Howard J. *How to Prosper During the Coming Bad Years.* New York: Times Books, 1979.

2. Toynbee, Arnold. *Surviving the Future.* London, 1971.

13

Living in a Surveillance Society

We are slowly awakening to the fact that we have lost our most basic rights of freedom, as Big Brother government increasingly monitors our lives. For the first time in history, the average citizen can no longer assume that his personal conversations in a public place (such as an airport or on the telephone) are secure from government eavesdropping. The technology of surveillance has made surprising advances in the last decade, and the government's war on drugs, terrorism, and money laundering has created the political will to permit the widespread surveillance of citizens. The result of this combination of high-tech surveillance and the need to focus on the activities of dangerous individuals in our democracy, has led to the creation of a "fish bowl" existence, eliminating both privacy and the freedom to be left alone that most humans have enjoyed throughout history, until now.

Mount Weather: The Headquarters of the U.S. Secret Government

Progressive Magazine published an article in March 1976 called "The Mysterious Mountain," describing the top-secret government installation known as Mount Weather, a facility designed to maintain government control of the United States after a nuclear war or other major disaster seriously affects the infrastructure of the United States. Richard Pollock developed his in-depth investigative piece from extensive Senate subcommittee hearings and interviews with military and civilian officials who were willing to discuss the situation "off the record." Pollock's report and a 1991 article in *TIME* magazine called "Doomsday Hideaway" provide fascinating information about the plans of the government to survive a future disaster.

Mount Weather was constructed during the most dangerous years of the Cold War deep inside a granite mountain not far from the small town of Bluemont, Virginia, approximately fifty miles outside of Washington, D.C. Mount Weather is also known by its official title, the Western Virginia Office of Controlled Conflict Operations. Ted Gup, a *TIME* reporter, wrote that "Mount Weather is a virtually self-contained facility. Above ground, scattered across manicured lawns, are about a dozen buildings bristling with antennas and microwave relay systems. An on-site sewage-treatment plant, with a 90,000 gallon-a-day capacity, and two tanks holding 250,000 gal. of water could last some 200 people more than a month; underground ponds hold additional water supplies. . . . The mountain's real secrets are not visible at ground level." Apparently the level of security surrounding the base is very high. Anyone approaching the area is detained, and any film of the area is destroyed. Originally, Mount Weather was used in the 1930s and 1940s as a National Weather Bureau Facility (hence its name).

People who have worked there in the past describe Mount Weather as an underground city, equipped with apartments and dormitories, cafeterias, hospitals, and self-contained utilities for water, sewage, and power. Apparently, it also contains its own television facilities and mass-transit system. This underground center is the command center for the Federal Emergency Management Agency (FEMA), which oversees more than one hundred Federal Relocation Centers in Pennsylvania, Virginia, Maryland, and North Carolina. Pollock's article reveals that these underground facilities are the center of the government's Continuity of Government program. The executive orders passed by various presidents provide that, in a national emergency such as a nuclear war or a vast national disaster, the president and top officials in the executive branch of the government would be transferred to this safe haven.

Researchers found that the U.S. Congress has almost no detailed knowledge about the functions or purposes of this national security installation. In 1975, a hearing of the Senate Subcommittee on Constitutional Rights received testimony from Air Force General (Retired) Leslie W. Bray about Mount Weather. Bray stated, "I am not at liberty to describe precisely what is the role and the mission and the capability that we have at Mount Weather, or at any other precise location."

New Technologies of Surveillance

Surveillance cameras now constantly monitor our highways, streets, parking lots, and buildings. They fundamentally alter our way of life. Our privacy is being progressively eroded by new technologies. During a recent trip to Britain and Scotland, I noticed that surveillance cameras were mounted above street lamps and on the sides of many skyscrapers, allowing the cameras to monitor all activities in the street or alley ways. Discussions with security people revealed that these cameras and the parabolic microphones that work in conjunction with them allow police security officials to monitor the actions of citizens twenty-four hours a day. In the event of a burglary, these films result in fast convictions or plea bargains that send felons to jail. As a consequence of the widespread introduction of these high-tech security surveillance systems throughout the cities and towns of the United Kingdom, the citizens have seen a welcome reduction in street muggings and burglaries. However, citizens must now walk the streets with the full knowledge that their every word and action is potentially under the watchful eye of Big Brother government. These very effective security cameras are coming to a city near you.

How do you feel about government officials, the police, or other inquisitive individuals knowing every detail of your private life? The complete record of your travel destinations, your choice of books, newspapers, movies, pay-TV choices, your traffic tickets, your medical tests, and every purchase you make is now electronically recorded and "on file" for anyone who can access these computer records. The technical capability of the government to monitor every aspect of your life eliminates your ability to protect your privacy. Despite the growing public concern with the issue of privacy of our computer records, the governments of the United States and Canada have totally failed to protect their citizens from privacy intrusions. Recently, an Australian supermarket chain threw out their old employee time clocks and replaced them with sophisticated fingerprint scanners that prevent employees from having friends cover for them if they want to skip out of work early.

The End of Privacy

A *TIME* magazine article by David Van Biema reported that the U.S. Department of Justice had funded research on the development of security scanners that police could use from a distance to scan a crowd in order to detect anyone on the street who is carrying a concealed gun. One of these devices measures variations in the natural electromagnetic field that surrounds a person, which is distorted by the presence of a metal weapon. Another device sends out pulsed radiation that is reflected back to a mobile scanner. A computer device on the mobile scanner can actually detect the difference between a knife and a revolver. These devices, costing less than $10,000, would allow a street patrol to determine if possible suspects are armed before approaching them.

Researchers at AT&T's Bell Labs in Baltimore, New Jersey, demonstrated a new scanning device on May 25, 1995 to a Conference on Lasers and Electro-Optics. The apparatus generates T-rays (terahertz, or trillion-cycle-per-second, electromagnetic pulses) that can be focussed on an object or human subject from a distance. When these rays reflect back to the device, they alter their frequency slightly, depending on the chemical makeup of the object scanned. This change in frequency can be analyzed to determine precisely what the object is. For example, it can examine luggage on a conveyer belt in an airport and instantly detect the presence of hidden explosives, drugs, or weapons. Its precision makes it possible for a manufacturer to instantly examine a metal part and see inside the metal to detect dangerous weaknesses. The possible security applications of this system are unlimited. However, these sophisticated scanners also affect your privacy, if you or your property is of interest to the police or intelligence agencies.

The Loss of Our Civil Rights and Freedom

The U.S. Bill of Rights provides protection against government harassment through its constitutional guarantee of "freedom from unreasonable search and seizure." The Fourth Amendment to the U.S. Constitution declares, "The right of the people to be secure in their persons, houses, papers, and effects, against unreasonable searches and seizures, shall not be violated." However, the U.S. Supreme Court ruled in 1990 that police checkpoints to apprehend drunks are legal. Police can now place roadblocks to intercept cars and interrogate all drivers. Despite the fact that studies show that 99 percent of drivers are not drinking, police can now demand that all drivers submit to sobriety tests. Additionally, they can search cars if they choose to do so. These police actions are more in line with the practices of dictatorial police states than the police activities that Americans have taken for granted over the last two hundred years. These police actions that assume citizens are guilty until proven innocent are consistent with the government's practice of secretly monitoring all of our bank accounts, our deposits and withdrawals, to discover the one-tenth of 1 percent of citizens who are money launderers or drug dealers. These intrusive procedures and legal assumptions are a total reversal of the basic legal philosophy of "the presumption of innocence" that has defined our North American democracies for the last two centuries.

Computer Surveillance

Although tens of millions of citizens surf the Internet for news, sports, and assorted research facilities every day, very few of them are aware that much of what they do on the Internet is being secretly monitored by both corporate Web site operators, and possibly government intelligence organizations and police agencies. When you visit a Web site, the creator of that site may very likely have constructed what is known as a "cookie" (a small piece of computer code that allows the Web site to identify various details about you that will allow the site to more easily facilitate your next visit). However, some cookie programs allow the Web site to instantaneously detect a great deal about their visitor, including the details of their computer system, their Internet provider, and even their personal identity. Some computer security experts have told me that intelligence agencies can target a particular Internet customer and literally build a map of every one of the sites that person visits over the years.

There is an Internet site called DejaNews that actually allows other Internet customers to enter a person's name and trace every newsgroup that that person has visited since 1990 and read the various comments he or she made over the years. Anyone who uses the Internet should operate on the assumption that they have someone looking over their shoulder at all times. Ominously, several very knowledgeable computer experts have warned that there are Web sites that, if visited, allow the operator of that Web site to actually invade your computer's hard drive and observe everything that is on your hard drive while you are connected to the site.

Surveillance Technology in the Workplace

The use of security cameras is expanding to include the surveillance of employees at their desks, in washrooms, and throughout the factory or store. Many computer administrators are able to monitor every single keystroke of thousands of employees and measure their job performance. The strong corporate arguments in favor of such continuous employee and customer monitoring include crime prevention, protection of staff, and employee drug-prevention programs. A new security device utilizes a suede type of cloth that an employer or parent can wipe over a computer keyboard or dresser top in order to absorb the invisible oils deposited by the fingertips of a keyboard user or teenager. When the specially treated cloth is sent to the company's laboratory for analysis, they will report back in ten days with a full evaluation indicating the detection or presence of up to twenty different drugs, including marijuana, cocaine, or alcohol. Many employees are now living a secretly monitored life that is little different from that described by George Orwell in his frightening novel *1984*.

The widespread introduction of corporate security systems requiring all workers to wear an employee badge containing an implanted computer microchip has given companies the potential to monitor the location and activity of every worker. As the employee enters his office, the computer records the exact time. Sensors placed at strategic locations throughout the building will record the location and duration of every movement by the badge wearer. New sophisticated office phone systems allow your boss to listen in on any private phone calls you might make. Many computerized office phone systems contain a record of all possible legitimate business phone numbers. If an employee places a personal call to a friend, the office phone system will record the unauthorized number and produce a report of these private calls and their duration, providing ammunition for his supervisor at his next evaluation interview.

The International Labor Organization in Geneva recently warned, "Workers in industrialized countries are losing privacy in the work place as technological advances allow employers to monitor nearly every facet of time on the job." The study claimed that the United States was the worst offender. Recently, the American Civil Liberties Union stated, "Criminals have more privacy rights than employees. Police have to get a court order, whereas in the work place, surveillance can be conducted without safeguards." Employees often complain about the incredible job stress they experience, knowing that they are being monitored every minute of the day. In many companies, the use of random drug testing and secret cameras, as well as intrusive psychological questionnaires, is creating a very unhealthy psychological environment of constant suspicion.

It is now possible to set up a microwave transmitter up to one mile outside a target building and focus its beams at a window. As the individuals within the room speak, the window of the office will vibrate imperceptibly. These vibrations can actually be detected by the microwave as the beams reflect off the window and then be reassembled into a muffled, but understandable conversation.

Several friends in the field of private investigations and industrial counterespionage have shown me some of these incredible surveillance devices. A new pinhole camera can be placed behind a wall that can monitor the next room audibly and visually. It is almost impossible to detect the tiny lens, unless you examine every wall, floor, and ceiling surface with a magnifying glass. These new cameras can photograph, silently, in almost total darkness. Another new surveillance camera is secretly concealed in a small mobile telephone, with the camera lens recording through the tiny hole normally used for the microphone. During a negotiation, the owner can leave the phone in a boardroom when he leaves the room. As the other team discusses their negotiating position "in private," the other party can secretly record everything being discussed.

Surveillance devices that enable you to monitor everything occurring in your home or office while you are away can now be purchased for several hundred dollars. One remote monitoring device, the XPS-1000, allows you to call your phone number from anywhere in the world by dialing your phone with a special activation code. The device will not ring your phone; however, from that moment on, you can monitor every sound in the building. Another tiny apparatus, a microtransmitter surveillance bug powered for three months by a miniature battery, can be used to secretly broadcast, up to one thousand yards, to a radio receiver on any FM frequency you have chosen. Privacy is now an illusion. If someone truly is determined to monitor your activities, they can do it.

Every single computer emits or leaks electromagnetic radiation (EMR) from its cathode ray tube, as well as from several of its components, including cables and spinning hard drive. Decades ago the U.S. government realized that a sophisticated computer device could be set up within a range of several hundred yards of any such computer and, when correctly tuned to match the electromagnetic radiation from the target computer, could actually cause the bits of information that appear on the monitor screen of the target computer to be duplicated precisely on the surveillance monitor. As a result, whatever appears on the screen of the target computer can be read by the intelligence specialist. More sophisticated devices developed by U.S. research labs can read the data on a spinning hard drive using variations of this technology. The passive nature of the eavesdropping for EMR emissions makes it impossible for anyone to detect that someone is spying on them.

The Identification Technology Revolution

Following several tragic incidents of babies being stolen from maternity wards, hospitals worldwide are exploring technologies that will make it increasingly difficult for an unauthorized person to leave a hospital with a newborn baby. The *Edinburgh Evening News* reported on June 20, 1994 that babies at Edinburgh's Capital Hospital now have a miniature electronic monitor attached to the snug wristband that encircles the tiny wrist of the smallest baby. If someone attempts to take the baby away from the controlled maternity areas, an alarm will summon the hospital security staff. The paper reported that "police have welcomed the use of the lightweight, washable device currently undergoing trials at Simpson Memorial Maternity pavilion. . . . It is the latest in new-age child protection, developed to stall kidnap bids." Of course, a determined kidnapper will find some method to remove the electronic monitor from the child's wrist. The final solution to this problem will probably involve a permanent and non-removable miniaturized computer chip that can be inserted beneath the skin of the newborn baby. In addition to protecting babies from kidnapping, such an identification device would provide lifelong ID for police, health, and possibly, financial purposes. Patients in several South Korean hospitals are now implanted with tiny computer ID chips in their fingertips as a foolproof identification system. Nurses with an electronic scanner can verify their identity to prevent an operation on the wrong patient.

The New Technology of Magnetic Fingerprints

Scientists have discovered that just as humans have unique fingerprints, all magnetic media, credit cards, computer hard drives, and electronic security pass cards possess unique magnetic properties at the microscopic level. These minute differences can be detected, recorded, and used to identify whether or not a particular credit or security card is an original or counterfeit. With banks losing over $1 billion every year to credit card counterfeiters, there is a significant motive to develop magnetic fingerprints that can provide absolutely secure identification. We are rapidly approaching the day when the government will be able to track every single citizen from the cradle to the grave, with no possibility of anyone escaping the electronic surveillance net. This unique magnetic characteristic of individual computer components allows investigators to focus their surveillance on any particular target computer, even if it exists within a room filled with dozens of other computers.

Control of Illegal Aliens and a National Identity Card

The growing concern in the United States about the millions of illegal immigrants entering the country without valid green cards is leading to the development of employment surveillance systems. Many in Congress want to introduce a national immigration smart card with a computer chip that provides proof that an individual has the legal right to work in the United States. New laws require employers to check with the federal government to make certain that a prospective employee is a legal resident or citizen. As these and similar laws are passed, the FBI and the police are beginning to achieve their long-term goal of registering all American citizens in a national identification database. This will enable the government to monitor the actions of every citizen. All dictatorships require their citizens to carry their "national identification card" at all times. The immigration card that is proposed will be a smart card—an identification card containing a computer chip that can electronically encode unique biometric and personal information. This encoded biometric information may include your fingerprints, your handprint, or your unique voiceprint, which will instantly provide positive identification. This technology will also prevent the counterfeiting of cards.

The pressure is growing to expand the information contained in such a national identification card to include a Social Security Number, immigration records, and possibly police files. Consider the vastly expanded uses for the Social Security card, even though the government originally promised that it would never be used for identification purposes.

A National Identification Center

The White House and the Congress secretly agreed to build a National Identification Center in Virginia. This center will enable federal law enforcement and intelligence agencies to collect vast amounts of data on an advanced computer system. Sophisticated computers will record and consolidate the hundreds of existing computer records the government possesses on every citizen. Ostensibly, this new identification center will be used primarily to monitor the compliance of citizens with new gun control regulations. However, the benefits of a national computer center containing data files on every American are obvious for those in the elitist government circles who wish ultimately to establish their police control over America.

Congressman Neal Smith, from Iowa's fourth district, revealed the government's secret plans to his constituents in his October 1993 newsletter. While discussing the handgun control laws that he supports, Smith claimed responsibility for helping to create this National Identification Center that will be used to monitor citizens for gun control and "other" purposes. In his newsletter, he said the following:

> The Subcommittee on Appropriations which I chair has been actively pursuing an effective solution to this problem. . . . But the program we are implementing will take more time. The solution to screening people . . . is to have a National Center computerized so that local law enforcement offices can instantly access information from all states. In other words, all states that supply that information to the National Center will have a positive identification system which will identify any applicant. . . . We have invested $392 million so far in such a Center, about a four-hour drive from Washington, D.C., and we hope to have it completed and equipped in about two years. . . . We hope all states will be in the system by 1998 and will supply the information on a continuing basis. . . . Meanwhile, we will continue to establish the National Identification Center for this and other law enforcement purposes.

The National Identification Center will allow all

governmental intelligence agencies, including the ATF and FBI, to identify and monitor all registered gun owners. But what are the "other law enforcement purposes" they intend to pursue? This National Identification Center is only one component of an all-encompassing system of police control that is being established nationwide. The super-secret government agencies—the National Reconnaissance Office and the National Security Agency —now have the capability to monitor phone calls and fax transmission worldwide.

During the year-long hunt for the Colombian drug lord Pabulo Esctavar, U.S. intelligence agencies scanned and monitored the Colombian telephone system and South American radio bands for any call containing Esctavar's voice. After almost a year of silence, Esctavar made the fatal mistake of speaking on the phone for about thirty seconds. Within ten seconds of beginning his call, NSA intelligence specialists were able to select his voice out of hundreds of thousands of simultaneous phone calls throughout South America through voiceprint analysis. Every human voice has a unique "voice signature" that is as individual as a person's fingerprints. If the intelligence agencies have a recording of you speaking for less than one minute, they can isolate your unique voiceprint from millions of other voices. Government agents instantly targeted Pabulo Esctavar's voice and triangulated the precise location of his phone. Within minutes the Colombian police commandos stormed his hideout and killed him.

The iris is as unique as your fingerprint. New surveillance technologies include the ability of camera systems to photograph the iris of the human eye from up to one hundred yards away and identify anyone. One such iris identification system—selling for $1,400—is manufactured by Biometric Identification Inc. in Los Angeles. In 1998, the company will introduce a monitoring device the size of a quarter that can be installed within a bank's automatic teller system to positively identify a customer without the need for a PIN number. These miniature iris detectors can be installed in high-security computer systems or defense installations to assure top-security access to only those who should have access. A report in the Canadian newspaper, *The Toronto Sun*, describes plans by Canadian banks to adopt a check thumbprint system that will validate the identity of any non-bank-account customer that wants to cash a check. Such systems have been used for years by some American banks.

The Clipper Chip Proposal

Over the last decade, elaborate and effective encryption programs have been developed that are now widely available to businessmen, professionals, other citizens concerned with providing some measure of security from spying competitors, foreign industrial intelligence operatives, and nosy neighbors. Programs such as Pretty Good Privacy allow the average citizen to protect his critical computer data, telephone calls, and email messages. Properly encrypted messages cannot be broken by anyone unless he has access to the sophisticated and extremely powerful supercomputers of the U.S. National Security Agency (NSA). These commercially available encryption programs are so effective that anyone other than the NSA would need over a year to break the encryption.

In addition to eavesdropping on our phone calls, the government wants to introduce the "clipper chip," which will allow intelligence agencies and the FBI to unlock the secret encryption codes of every communication system and computer program in America. Over the last decade, mathematicians have developed sophisticated mathematical encryption programs that allow the average business owners or computer users to safely encrypt their confidential information so that no one can read their private files. This clipper chip program will provide police and intelligence agencies with a "back door" to break your encryption code and read your confidential files. The clipper chip is now being installed in telephones, TVs, and other consumer electronic products throughout America. The government has already invested $500 million in technologies (digital communications and fiber optics the size of a human hair that can carry a million phone calls simultaneously) that ensure its ability to monitor your private telephone calls with impunity. In Canada, the super-secret Communications Security Establishment (CSE) has received permission to continue surveillance of Canada's federal communication system and decode advanced computer encryption codes used by businesses and individuals.

Living in a Surveillance Society

As I reported in my books *Prince of Darkness* and *Final Warning*, the National Security Agency has denied that it can listen to all phone calls and radio messages throughout the world. However, Mike Frost, a former interception intelligence specialist working with the Canadian Communications Security Establishment, is one of several intelligence sources that has confirmed that the NSA has this intelligence capability. Mike Frost was trained during the 1980s at the special National Security Agency school outside Washington, D.C., where he was taught to install sophisticated listening devices on the roofs of U.S. embassies and other sites worldwide. Frost admitted to *The Toronto Sun* newspaper that he installed these devices in many national capitals to monitor communications and phone calls worldwide. In North America, the NSA phone surveillance program code name is called "Oratory." In Britain, the BBC reported that the MI-6 interception technology is called the "Dictionary Program." Their Cray supercomputers record and monitor millions of our phone calls and simultaneously listen for the use of any of four hundred key words that have been programmed into the computer system.

If a phone caller uses one or more key words in his conversation (such as explosive, bomb, gas, gun, drugs, White House), the computer will record that particular phone call for later analysis. During the following day, a human intelligence specialist operator will analyze that phone call to determine if the call has any significance for national security purposes. Obviously, the vast majority of the monitored phone calls will not contain the key words and will be immediately dumped without being listened to by a human operator. However, if the call is of interest to the intelligence agencies, they will thereafter monitor all future calls to and from that particular phone number. When this monitoring capability is integrated with voiceprint analysis, the National Security Agency can instantly identify and monitor the phone calls of any targeted individual within five seconds of the moment they commence speaking from any phone on earth. While I am concerned with this technology (as one who loves privacy and freedom), I believe that our governments have no choice today but to monitor all communications; we live in a world where terrorists can destroy a city's population with Sarin nerve gas or a possible nuclear warhead. However, our privacy has been forever lost.

14

Financial Strategies in Light of the Y2K Crisis

Christians should have a balanced and biblically based attitude about their finances, especially in light of the growing dangers the Y2K crisis presents. We need to recognize that our financial resources are simply a tool that the Lord has placed in our hands as a trust to be administered. Someday, each of us will give the Lord an accounting of our stewardship of the finances He has entrusted to us.

Our Attitude Toward Finances

Many Christians have never evaluated their attitude toward money and financial planning according to the Word of God. As a consequence, they often possess erroneous and harmful attitudes that hinder their financial success and peace of mind. Some people believe that we should passively wait for God to protect us, that there is little need for financial or practical preparations to protect against emergencies or disasters such as Y2K. Some spiritualize their procrastination and justify their lack of financial planning in the belief that God will somehow protect them, regardless of their lack of foresight and preparations. However, the Lord commands us to provide for the needs of our families.

Finance is one of the areas where the attitudes of man and God differ markedly. Ultimately, we need to evaluate our attitudes toward our finances and possessions in respect to the Word of God. Are we truly the owners of the property and money that pass through our hands? Or are we to regard our property and income with the attitude of a steward who has been entrusted with valuable possessions that he administers for the true owner— God—who will someday demand a full accounting? As Christians, the answer is clear. All we own and all that we shall ever possess should be held lightly; our possessions are not our own. We are just passing through this life. Our eternal destiny is in heaven. The Lord commands us, "Lay not up for yourselves treasures upon earth, where moth and rust doth corrupt, and where thieves break through and steal: But lay up for yourselves treasures in heaven, where neither moth nor rust doth corrupt, and where thieves do not break through nor steal" (Matt. 6:19-20). In the words of Christ, "For what is a man profited, if he gains the whole world, and loses his own soul? Or what will a man give in exchange for his soul?" (Matt. 16:26). The Word of God reminds us that "a man's life consisteth not in the abundance of the things which he possesseth" (Luke 12:15).

When we examine the Scriptures, we discover a number of biblical principles that should guide us in preparing for possible contingencies in light of the approaching Y2K crisis. As in every area of our Christian life, we need to find the biblically balanced position based on "the whole counsel of God."

The Need for Diligence and Prudent Preparations

Throughout the Scriptures God commands us to be diligent and prudent with our finances. It is interesting to note that you cannot find a single biblical hero who is weak, indecisive, or lazy. While it is God who prospers our efforts, He expects us to do our part. In the book of Proverbs, we find a number of passages that describe this principle. "Be thou diligent to know the state of thy flocks, and look well to thy herds" (Prov. 27:23). The Scriptures promise God's blessing, if we diligently and faithfully work to accomplish our task. "He that tilleth his land shall have plenty of bread"

(Prov. 28:19). The Word of God commends our diligent efforts to prepare for our future needs. "Go to the ant, thou sluggard; consider her ways, and be wise" (Prov. 6:6). The Bible instructs us as follows: "But this I say, He which soweth sparingly shall reap also sparingly; and he which soweth bountifully shall reap also bountifully" (2 Cor. 9:6). Once we have faithfully and diligently done our part, we can prayerfully ask the Lord to bless our efforts and give us wisdom regarding how we can best protect our family.

God Will Supply Our Needs

"But my God shall supply all your need according to his riches in glory by Christ Jesus" (Phil. 4:19). One of the most fundamental of biblical truths is that God is vitally concerned with our practical, daily economic needs. The pages of Scripture contain a complete set of principles that should undergird our basic financial strategies during these last days, when the world is at risk of a major economic collapse if millions of computers across the globe fail. While we await the Resurrection, which could occur at any moment, we must realize that the Lord may delay His return for many years, and therefore we must be prepared to "occupy till He comes." If the Lord tarries for a number of years, we may have to live through the economic roller-coaster crisis just ahead. Therefore, we need to understand that our ultimate source is not our salary or our investment savings, but, rather, our Father in heaven. He will guide us through His Word and through His Holy Spirit to know what we need to do to protect ourselves, our families, and our churches. King David described God's unchanging faithfulness to His children: "I have been young, and now am old; yet have I not seen the righteous forsaken, nor his seed begging bread" (Ps. 37:25).

Although God has promised to care for us, in the parable of the servants and the talents the Lord instructed us to practically invest the resources He has placed in our hands to provide for the needs of our lives and our family. The two faithful servants who invested their talents to gain a positive return were commended and honored for their faithfulness. The servant who passively hid his one talent in the ground was severely reprimanded by his master for his laziness and lack of stewardship. The master of the unfaithful servant told him, "Thou wicked and slothful servant, thou knewest that I reap where I sowed not, and gather where I have not sowed: Thou oughtest therefore to have put my money to the exchangers, and then at my coming I should have received mine own with usury. Take therefore the talent from him, and give it unto him which hath ten talents. For unto every one that hath shall be given, and he shall have abundance: but from him that hath not shall be taken away even that which he hath" (Matt. 25:26-29). This teaching of our Lord clearly commands us to be good stewards of our resources.

The Word of God informs us, "For the love of money is the root of all evil: which while some coveted after, they have erred from the faith, and pierced themselves through with many sorrows" (1 Tim. 6:10). Those who are obsessed with money are not walking in the will of God. However, we should not misunderstand this command. It isn't money itself that is the root of evil. It is the overwhelming "love of money" that is sinful. Many passages in the Scriptures command us to act with prudence, diligence, hard work, and to make wise investments. God commended the faithfulness and financial stewardship of Abraham, Isaac, Jacob, and many others (such as Job) after their trials. As Christians, we need to handle our possessions and finances faithfully and prayerfully, in light of the knowledge that we will someday give an accounting to our Lord Jesus Christ.

Get Out of Debt Quickly

While debt for things such as a home mortgage or a business loan may be unavoidable, I strongly suggest that you attempt to get out of debt as quickly as possible. Those who owe a great deal of money are placing themselves under a certain level of financial bondage. Although you may not be able to pay off all your debts before the beginning of the next century, the less you owe, the less your life will be under the control of others. I suggest that you pay off all of your loans that you obtained for consumer items (including cars), if that is possible. As we enter the year 2000, those who owe substantial amounts to financial institutions may find that they are at the mercy of a corporation in chaos. For example, if your employer cannot pay you in early 2000, your failure to make timely loan payments might allow the bank to call your loan. Any personal financial difficulty may put you at the mercy of a bank desperate to resolve its own money problems.

Tithing and Firstfruits to the Lord

In the Old Testament, we find God's command to the Jews to pay a tithe—or 10 percent—to the temple in Jerusalem as an acknowledgment that they owed everything to the Lord. As Christians, we are living in the age of grace and are not subject to the old law; however, the divine principle of bringing our firstfruits to the Lord is still applicable to believers in the Church age. "Honour the Lord with thy substance, and with the firstfruits of all thine increase: So shall thy barns be filled with plenty" (Prov. 3:9-10). When we give God 10 percent as the firstfruits of our income, we are simply recognizing that the Lord really owns 100 percent of all we possess.

The Bible instructs us to pay our tithes to the local church, "the storehouse" where we are being spiritually fed and blessed. The prophet Malachi gave this command of God in the closing book of the Old Testament. "Bring ye all the tithes into the storehouse, that there may be meat in mine house, and prove me now herewith, saith the Lord of hosts, if I will not open you the windows of heaven, and pour you out a blessing, that there shall not be room enough to receive it" (Mal. 3:10). God has promised that He will bless us abundantly if we will be faithful to Him with our tithes. After eighteen years as a professional financial planner, I found that almost every financially successful Christian I know has learned by experience that we simply cannot give more to the Lord than He will return to us. Tithing is one of the fundamental principles we need to establish in our financial planning as a priority. As a Christian, it is the most important key to your financial prosperity.

Providing for Others

Another key principle for our financial prosperity is the willingness to give to others in need. The apostle John wrote, "But whoso hath this world's good, and seeth his brother have need, and shutteth up his bowels of compassion from him, how dwelleth the love of God in him? My little children, let us not love in word, neither in tongue; but in deed and in truth" (1 John

3:17-18). Your attitude toward your money is a reflection of your attitude toward the Lord. The Christian who constantly blesses those around him will find himself blessed by God. Too often we think of giving only in terms of placing money in the offering plate or donating to a registered charitable fund. However, we need to be practical in our preparations for the Year 2000 crisis to gather resources that will be able to assist our brothers and sisters in Christ, as well as needy neighbors, in addition to our own family. "The liberal soul shall be made fat: and he that watereth shall be watered also himself" (Prov. 11:25).

A Year 2000 Study Group

In addition to practical physical assistance, in terms of things like sharing water and food, we should seriously consider the possibility of assisting fellow believers and neighbors by sharing knowledge of the coming crisis while there is time to make practical preparations. It might be very helpful to form a Year 2000 crisis study group, made up of interested members of your extended family or church group. Such a group could exchange and discuss Y2K material that group members acquire from the Internet, books, and articles. Giving this book to a friend may be the best way to awaken loved ones to the need to prepare for the Year 2000.

A Hedge of Protection around Your Family

In the midst of the growing economic panic as people awaken to the Year 2000 dangers surrounding us today, it would be easy for many Christians to lose their sense of peace and surrender to despair. However, as believers, we can confidently look to the Lord to protect us from unusual dangers. The Bible tells us that God made "a hedge around" Job as one of His faithful servants. Since God's nature is unchanging, we understand that the Lord still watches over each of His followers. While this does not guarantee that we will not suffer during the devastating economic and infrastructure breakdowns that lie ahead, we do know that as Christians we are under the Lord's watchful protection. Nothing terrible can happen to us without God allowing it in His permissive will. Satan acknowledged God's supernatural protection of His servant Job, in the following words: "Hast not thou made an hedge about him, and about his house, and about all that he hath on every side? thou hast blessed the work of his hands, and his substance is increased in the land" (Job 1:10). While God expects us to be diligent and prudent, ultimately our finances and our economic destiny lie in His Hands.

The Lord promised Israel great economic blessings if they would follow in obedience to His commands. "And the Lord shall make thee plenteous in goods, in the fruit of thy body, and in the fruit of thy cattle, and in the fruit of thy ground, in the land which the LORD sware unto thy fathers to give thee. The Lord shall open unto thee his good treasure, the heaven to give the rain unto thy land in his season, and to bless all the work of thine hand: and thou shalt lend unto many nations, and thou shalt not borrow" (Deut. 28:11-12).

The most important principle we can follow regarding our financial and practical preparations for the year 2000 is to place our trust in our heavenly Father, prudently follow His biblical principles, and ask Him to direct our path. "Trust in the Lord with all thine heart; and lean not unto thine own understanding. In all thy ways acknowledge him, and he shall direct thy paths" (Prov. 3:5-6).

The Goal: Financial Survival After the Year 2000

Financial survival in the Year 2000 crisis can be attained by accumulating an amount of spendable capital to guarantee the essential income to meet your family's basic survival needs without having to depend on government resources. Financial survival is a practical goal that can be achieved by most of us if we apply some principles of disaster planning and conservative finance. As you work consistently towards your goal, beginning as soon as possible, you should be able to arrange your financial affairs to provide the necessary spendable cash (plus gold and silver coins) to enable your family to survive if the banks and the ATM machines close. We will examine several strategies to preserve and protect yourself against the special financial risks in the early months of the year 2000.

The reason the majority of people may be left without financial options after January 1, 2000 is the natural tendency to deny that the Y2K problem could actually close the banking system and disrupt most of our lives for a few months. Those who will suffer because they have not made practical preparations will not have planned to fail; they may simply have failed to develop and follow a plan for financial survival.

For most people, the most practical solution will be to slowly, over the coming months between now and December 31, 1999, withdraw as much in cash out of their bank account (or their monthly paycheck in cash) as they can. It is important that you not take more than $10,000 out in cash at any one time. The banking regulations demand that a Currency Transaction Report be filled out by the bank (and sent to the IRS) reporting anyone withdrawing more than $10,000 in cash at any one time. The principle is simple, but fundamental, from this point on. Until the start of the new millennium, when you cash your paycheck, pay yourself first by withdrawing a certain amount in cash every month, and safely store this cash in a safe place.

While you may feel that it will be difficult to store a certain amount in cash every month, the truth is that you cannot afford to delay. The possibility of a serious run on the banks, beginning in 1999, is very real. Unless you begin today, you may find that at some point in 2000, your life savings are tied up in the bank's lost computer files, which may take months to recover. The key to financially surviving the Year 2000 crisis is to begin today.

Investment Options Between Now And January 1, 2000

Government Savings Bonds

One of the safest and easiest investment choices for the very conservative investor, between now and the fall of 1999, is an investment in government savings bonds offered by either the U.S. and/or Canadian governments. While these investments are normally seen as appropriate only for three to five year periods, in the unprecedented risks we face between now and the end of December 1999, these government-backed bonds represent one place where you can safely park a large amount of your life savings that you decide to remove from the stock market or from mutual funds because of the perceived risk of a stock market collapse as the dimensions of the Year 2000 computer crisis begin to be felt in the world's stock markets. While you would normally think of parking larger amounts of your savings in your local bank, the dangers of a huge run on the banks at any time during 1999 leads me to suggest that you consider other options for a temporary parking place.

Since these government savings bonds are backed by the taxation power of the federal government, and since the government must pay the interest due if they wish to borrow additional funds in the future, these government savings bonds are almost without risk until the end of 1999. Government savings bonds can usually be purchased in various denominations from any financial institution. Some government savings bonds pay regular interest every year, while other savings bonds compound the interest over the duration of the bond. Usually, compound savings bonds provide a higher rate of return.

U.S. or Canadian Treasury Bills

Treasury Bills (T-bills) are federal government–backed investments, fully secured by the taxation authority of the federal government. T-bills are safe investments to park your investment funds until we reach the late fall of 1999. They are investment vehicles in which an investor lends the government a significant amount of funds for a period of 91, 182, or 364 days at a competitive interest rate. T-bills have the same level of security as government savings bonds, but are usually available only in large denominations of $50,000 or more. Rather than paying an interest rate, T-bills are sold to the investor at a discount, and the government returns the full amount to you at maturity. The difference represents your interest return. For example, if you purchase a 180-day T-Bill for $97,000, six months later the government might pay you $100,000, depending on interest rates. This $3,000 gain (interest) is exempt from state and local taxes for Americans; however you are subject to federal income tax on these earnings.

Common Stocks and Mutual Funds

In the late 1990s, we are experiencing the greatest speculative stock market bubble in this century. I believe it is only a matter of time until there may be a major drop in the price of shares. As detailed in an earlier chapter, the stock market is poised for major losses, which could destroy the life savings of millions of North

Americans. This is a prescription for disaster. Stock and bond markets both are threatened by the volatile financial derivatives market (with $42 trillion at risk). The management teams running these mutual funds have abandoned many of the fundamental safeguards that were designed after the 1929 crash. These factors suggest that mutual funds are not a safe and secure place to put your funds at this time for the average conservative investor, especially in light of the dangers from the Y2K crisis.

We may be standing on the brink of a potential stock and bond market collapse that could wipe out the life savings of millions of investors. There is a growing awareness by the investing public of the unique and unprecedented dangers to both the stock market itself and the underlying profits of thousands of corporations that must spend tens of millions of dollars to fix their Y2K computer problems. If you are a professional investor, you will probably choose to take whatever risks seem to be appropriate to your situation. However, for the average investor who cannot afford to lose 20 or 40 percent of their investments in equities, I would strongly recommend that you prayerfully consider transferring your existing investment in stocks or your mutual funds into more conservative and secure investments (e.g., T-bills, money market funds, investment certificates, gold, and silver) as soon as possible, before the Y2K risks begin to impact share prices.

Money Market Funds

These investment funds are a form of mutual fund offered by stock brokers and other financial institutions. Money market funds invest your funds in short-term financial securities such as T-bills, bonds, or commercial short-term loans offered by corporations. Instead of owning a bond or T-bill directly, you, as an investor, will own a unit in the money market fund that itself owns the underlying T-bill, bond, etc. These money market funds calculate the interest generated by the fund's investments every day. These funds are very liquid but are subject to severe losses if interest rates change quickly. Despite the fact that millions of investors have entrusted their money to these money market funds, many investors do not realize that they are not protected by federal deposit insurance. The usual minimum investment may be in the range of one thousand dollars, with the earned interest either paid out to the investor every month or reinvested to purchase additional units of the fund.

Some people may want to park the money that they have withdrawn from their mutual funds or stocks into a money market fund between now and the fall of 1999, when they may definitely want to pull some of their money out in cash. While money market funds are extremely accessible to investors, they may be rather shaky investments in the year 2000, during the disruption of the entire financial system. One of the dangers in a money market fund is that you, as an investor, only own units or shares in the money market fund. The investor in the money market fund does not directly own the underlying financial security such as the government T-bill or savings bond. As some money market funds are investing in dangerous financial derivatives without the express knowledge of their fund investors, it may be wise to avoid such funds at this time. Consider investing directly in whatever investments you judge are appropriate (such as T-bills or federal government bonds) for your portfolio, considering the level of risk and possible rate of return.

Guaranteed Investment Certificates; Certificates of Deposit

Guaranteed Investment Certificates (GICs), or Certificates of Deposit (CDs), are sold by banks and other financial institutions as a short or medium-term investment. The advantage for most investors is the guaranteed rate of compound interest. The disadvantage is that your funds remain locked in for the duration of a term. It is essential that you check out the financial strength of the bank offering the GIC, especially in light of Y2K compliance.

Bank Term Deposits

Term deposits are offered by various financial institutions, including banks, as a vehicle to invest larger amounts ($5,000 and greater) for 90, 180, or 364 days. Term deposits tend to pay less interest than Guaranteed Investment Certificates, but they have the virtue of not being locked in. Term deposits can be surrendered for cash at any time before their maturity date, but a significant amount of interest may be lost as a penalty if you make an early withdrawal. However, term deposits issued by strong financial institutions offer excellent security. These are a good, safe place to put your investment funds for ninety days to six months while considering when you should pull all or most of your investment funds out of the financial institutions if you conclude that there is a real risk of many institutions failing as a result of the Year 2000 crisis.

Gold and Silver

One of the best financial investments to preserve the value of your assets is gold. First, governments cannot create gold at will, in the same way they print paper currency. Consequently, over the centuries gold has retained an almost constant value, while paper currencies have inevitably devalued. Throughout history, people have always relied on gold as the ultimate safeguard for their financial protection. Gold has the following characteristics: It is indestructible, compact, scarce, and portable.

Remarkably, Alan Greenspan, the chairman of the U.S. Federal Reserve Bank system, testified to Congress in February 1994 as follows:

> Gold is a different type of commodity because virtually all of the gold that has ever been produced still exists. . . . Therefore changes in the level of production have very little effect on the ongoing price, which means that it's virtually wholly a monetary demand phenomenon. It's a store of value measure which has shown a fairly consistent lead on inflation expectations, and has been over the years a reasonably good indicator. It does this better than commodity prices or a lot of other things.

A period of hyperinflation would almost certainly increase the value of gold and silver in the years ahead. Investing in gold and silver should not be viewed as a speculative investment, but rather as part of a survival strategy to assist in your plans to protect yourself and your family in the period after January 1, 2000. Gold and silver should not be purchased as a speculative investment for quick profits, but only as an insurance policy to provide guaranteed purchasing power at a time when the value of your banking accounts in your local bank may be uncertain.

Consider placing between 10 percent and 35 percent of your

normal investment funds in gold and silver coins, and possibly some bullion. The basic rationale for placing some of your investment funds in gold and silver is both prudence and insurance. For thousands of years, gold and silver have been the most stable and universal medium of exchange. In the early 1920s, a man could buy a good quality suit with an ounce of gold. Despite the enormous financial changes during the last eighty years, an ounce of gold will still buy a good quality suit today. Paper currency may be devalued if the government decides to produce vast amounts of paper currency in 1999. However, gold and silver remain in limited quantity; they will not lose their true value.

Those investors who wisely placed significant funds in gold and silver will be well rewarded. While the possession of gold bullion by Americans was made illegal by President Roosevelt in 1935, Americans could still legally own semi-numismatic gold coins because they were legal tender as coins. These coins now have collector value because of their relative rarity. Prudent American investors should hold any gold in the form of semi-numismatic coins rather than as gold bullion because of the historic experience of gold bullion confiscation during the 1930s.

President Ford introduced a law in 1974 that made possession of gold bullion legal again. Those who still choose to invest in gold bullion can purchase it in small units, bars, or wafers in various sizes. The advantages of gold bullion are its instant liquidity and universal negotiability. Since there is a charge for each bar on top of its actual price, it is to your advantage to buy the largest bar you can afford. Be sure the gold bar is stamped by a reputable refiner (such as Johnson Matthey or Handy & Harman) that will guarantee its purity (usually .9999 fine). I strongly recommend that you avoid responding to newspaper, TV, or mail ads offering to sell gold or silver. Many investors have lost their funds when they sent in checks to an advertisement and failed to receive the gold. Purchase your gold or silver coins or bullion from a large dealer or bank after shopping for the lowest commissions and bar charges.

A safety deposit box is recommended for storing any precious metal investment. However, once we approach the fall of 1999, I strongly recommend you should not store your valuables in your bank's safety deposit box because of the danger that the bank could fail or that your access to your safety deposit box could be limited for a period of months. As we approach the January 1, 2000, you would be wise to store all valuables (including your supply of spendable cash and gold or silver coins) in a strong safe or safety deposit box.

Gold or silver coins are most desirable because of their portability, universal liquidity, and negotiability. Among the most highly recommended one-ounce gold coins are the following: the Canadian Maple Leaf coin, the South African Krugerrand coin, and the American Eagle coin. In addition to the price of the gold, the coin's price will include a premium—10 percent or more for a one-tenth of an ounce coin, and 3.5 percent for a one-ounce coin. When you resell the gold coins you will recover some portion of the premium, but obviously, it is to your advantage to purchase larger coins to avoid excessive premium charges. Depending on the state or province you happen to live in, you also may have to pay sales tax on your gold purchase. I recommend that you consider purchasing your gold or silver coins from a reputable gold coin dealer or large financial institution after checking for the lowest premium available. Try to protect your precious coins from scratches that will reduce their value to a future purchaser. Don't leave your gold or silver coins, or bullion, in the possession of the gold bullion dealer in return for a certificate. It is vital that you demand physical delivery of your bullion or coins so that you can take physical possession of these valuable assets. Many investors have lost their complete investment when the dealer holding their coins subsequently went bankrupt.

American Citizens May Wish to Transfer IRA Funds

As the Y2K crisis becomes increasingly evident to the average citizen, many may want to consider transferring the funds within their IRAs or 401(k)s. Naturally, if you transfer your retirement funds outside your IRA, you may trigger both taxes and penalties, which makes this option undesirable in most cases.

However, it is possible to move your IRA retirement funds from the stock market and mutual funds into a more conservative investment, such as gold or silver bullion grade coins. The Internal Revenue Service allows an American to invest his IRA account funds in gold and silver coins as long as they are not collector grade coins. If you decide, after carefully analyzing your situation, that you want to place a portion of your investment funds in gold and silver coins as an insurance strategy to protect their value through the turmoil that may face the stock markets in the early days of the next millennium, then you might want to explore the following option.

I am indebted to Jim Lord's *Year 2000 Survival Newsletter* (Vol. 1, No. 4, December 31, 1997) for the following information. I highly recommend his book *A Survival Guide For the Year 2000 Problem*, as well as his newsletter. Information on how to obtain these resources is listed in the appendix.

According to IRS Publication 590 (pp. 35–36) regarding Individual Retirement Arrangements, the IRS rules allow a citizen to direct his investment into gold or silver bullion coins. In the section entitled Investment in Collectibles, the IRA rules prohibit most collectibles as useful IRA investments except for specific types of gold and silver coins. The text in this section reads as follows: "Exception: Your IRA can invest in one, one-half, one-quarter, or one-tenth ounce U.S. gold coins, or one-ounce silver coins minted by the Treasury Department."

Unfortunately, most qualified trustees of IRAs, including banks, mutual funds, and stock brokers, are not set up to handle these coin investments. Practically, if this option interests you, I would strongly suggest you talk to a competent attorney who is knowledgeable in this area and ask him to set up an IRA trust account into which you would transfer your existing assets. It is important to note that the attorney must retain control of the coins within the IRA tax-sheltered trust account. If you were to take possession of these coins, it would trigger the taxes and penalties you wish to avoid. In light of the dangers of many U.S. banks failing in the opening months of the year 2000, I would suggest that your lawyer not place these coins in a bank's safety deposit box. There are other choices, such as independent security deposit companies, that would be safer.

Canadians may wish to transfer some of their Registered Retirement Savings Account (RRSP) funds out of the stock market or equity mutual funds into more conservative investments that still qualify for their tax-sheltered RRSP. These investments include: Guaranteed Investment Certificates, Term Deposits, gold or silver coins. Another conservative investment in light of the Y2K crisis is to transfer your funds into a Balanced Mutual Fund that invests in safe federal government bonds and large Canadian companies.

The Risk of Hyperinflation if the Government Prints New Currency

There is a growing danger of hyperinflation in North America as we face the risk of runs on the bank due to fears of the Year 2000 computer crisis. If our governments attempt to flood the markets with cash by printing or releasing vast amounts of preprinted currency in their attempt to stop the runs on the bank, the government may hyperinflate the currency as the only possible method to produce the needed currency to keep the teller window open at the banks. However, the results of a decision to print vast amounts of currency and flood the banking system to stop the runs on the banks could be a wave of hyperinflation. Such government action could trigger growing wage demands, rapidly rising prices, and declining value of our North American currencies against the stronger Japanese and European currencies. The raging storm of hyperinflation could wipe out many investors.

Even if the government triggers hyperinflation to stave off the banking runs, there are still a few survival strategies available for the prudent investor. If you conclude that we are heading into a period of hyperinflation, sell your fixed long-term investments to become as liquid as possible. You may have to pay substantial surrender charges to withdraw your fixed-term funds. However, in a time of raging hyperinflation, if you hold on to investments in bonds, pensions, annuities, and fixed income funds, they may become almost worthless if the government hyper-inflates the currency.

Consider transferring a portion of your investment funds into precious metals, stable foreign currencies, and other conservative investments in countries that are not experiencing hyperinflation. As we approach the end of 1999, consider increasing your investment in precious metals from the typical 5 to10 percent to as much as 35 percent of your investment assets. As one example, the

Swiss franc, the currency of Switzerland, is still fully backed by gold and is therefore a strong and stable currency. An investment in a Swiss franc bank account, annuity or bond while paying a low conservative interest rate may provide the investor with unparalleled security in the financially dangerous times ahead. Keep in mind the wise phrase, "This too will pass." Even after a disastrous period of chaos and hyperinflation, the Y2K computer crisis will finally end and stability will return in the first few years of the new century. Those who have avoided huge losses and have retained their hard-won assets and cash by wisely shielding themselves from the devastating losses in failed banks, mutual funds, and the ravages of inflation will be in a position to purchase quality investments and real estate at phenomenal discounts.

15

Practical and Spiritual Strategies to Survive the Year 2000

Pray for the Best, Prepare for the Worst

How Do I Protect Myself and My Family from the Year 2000 Crisis?

It is vital that you respond to this approaching Year 2000 computer crisis with a well-planned strategy of practical and spiritual preparations. It is essential that you design a personal plan to protect yourself from the worst effects of this crisis. Pray for the best and prepare for the worst. In the following chapter I will recommend such a strategy.

The concept of preparedness is based on a mental and spiritual attitude of becoming aware of the possible dangers and responding to them with appropriate action. There are three aspects to Y2K preparedness:

1) *Spiritual Preparation.* This involves becoming aware of the spiritual principles that instruct us to prepare for the dangers that lie ahead, while ultimately depending on God for His guidance and protection.

2) *Preparation Planning.* This involves a willingness to examine the evidence of the dangers the Year 2000 crisis presents and to establish a plan to minimize the risks to your family, your home, and your finances.

3) *A Practical Home Storage Plan.* This plan involves a commitment to accumulate the necessary supplies of essential goods and foods that will allow your family to survive possible disruptions of food, water, and power in the first few months of the year 2000.

It is obvious that our modern generation does not plan for emergencies as our parents and grandparents did because we don't feel the urgencies of war, famine, plague, and earthquakes in the same way that they did. In past centuries, people felt that it was normal to plan and prepare for the disasters that would interfere with the functioning of society. However, technological advancements and stability of life in modern times have caused many of us to feel immune to disasters.

We have learned to take for granted the multitude of computer-controlled services and products that make our modern world so comfortable. We rely on twenty-four-hour ATMs, late-night supermarkets, convenience stores, and debit/credit cards that enable us to purchase whatever we need in almost any city of the industrialized world. Another factor that causes many of us to deny the possibility of disaster is the fact that many North Americans are living so close to the edge financially that they have little surplus funds to use to acquire the necessary survival food and materials required for disaster plans.

Spiritual Preparations

Throughout the Word of God our Lord commands His followers to take active preparations to protect ourselves and our families from the dangers that life presents. There are no verses in the Bible that suggest that Christians can simply ignore trouble ahead, expecting the Lord to supernaturally protect us. One example of the Bible's admonition to prepare for future trials and adversity can be found in the book of Proverbs. God commands us to emulate the practical ways of the lowly ant in providing for the future:

Go to the ant, thou sluggard; consider her ways, and be wise:

Which having no guide, overseer, or ruler,

Provideth her meat in the summer, and gathereth her food in the harvest.

How long wilt thou sleep, O sluggard? when wilt thou arise out of thy sleep?

Yet a little sleep, a little slumber, a little folding of the hands to sleep:

So shall thy poverty come as one that travelleth, and thy want as an armed man. (Prov. 6:6-11)

The Scriptures record God's command to His servant Joseph to advise the pharaoh of Egypt to take advantage of the seven years of plenty by storing precious grain foods for the approaching seven years of famine. The Bible clearly teaches us the principle of preparing for future disasters while maintaining our unshakable trust in God. However, as followers of Christ, we are not to allow ourselves to be full of worry or anxiety about the future.

Earlier in this book I noted God's strong command to exercise prudence and foresight in avoiding dangers. The book of Proverbs twice commanded us as follows: "A prudent man foreseeth the evil, and hideth himself: but the simple pass on, and are punished" (22:3 and 27:12).

Is It Right to Flee from Danger?

On many occasions the Word of God deals with the principle of taking action to escape danger or moving to another location to protect your loved ones from disaster or persecution. For example, Jesus commanded His disciples as follows: "But when they persecute you in this city, flee ye into another" (Matt. 10:23). The Scriptures record numerous examples of the people of God fleeing from persecutors or escaping before their enemies could do them bodily harm. This drastic action to flee from danger does not reflect a lack of faith on the part of God's people, but rather it is in keeping with the clear principles of using the mind God gave us to evaluate danger and take appropriate evasive action.

The Scriptures record numerous examples of this: Noah and his sons preparing the ark from the danger of the Flood; Abraham travelling to Egypt to escape the local famine in Palestine; Lot escaping from the wicked city of Sodom just before its destruction; and Moses escaping from Egypt and later his leading the Exodus of the whole people of Israel from slavery and death in Egypt. Later we read of the flight of David from King Saul and of the prophet Elijah escaping from the evil Queen Jezebel and Ahab. In the New Testament, Jesus escapes from those who wanted to stone him, and often travels with some secrecy. The epistles of the New Testament record numerous close escapes by the brave apostle Paul, who often was forced to escape by night over the city walls so he could faithfully continue his tremendous missionary journeys.

It is fascinating to note that Jesus Christ warned His disciples, in Matthew 24, to flee to the country when the Roman armies would begin a siege of Jerusalem. Thirty-eight years later the prophecy was fulfilled; the Roman armies besieged Jerusalem but broke off the siege for a few weeks. Tens of thousands of Jews immediately fled from the country into the seemingly impregnable city of Jerusalem whose walls were over a hundred feet high. However, every single Christian in the church in Jerusalem took advantage of the lull in the siege and fled from the city into the country and beyond in response to the prophesied warning of Jesus. As a consequence, according to the early Church, no Christians are known to have died in the fall of Jerusalem, when over one million were killed in A.D. 70. Although every mature Christian believer should be personally ready to die, if necessary, in the confidence that they will go to heaven to be with Christ, we are to use the wisdom and caution God gave us to protect our lives and loved ones.

In light of the tremendous problems posed by the Year 2000 computer crisis, I believe that we have a duty to awaken those around us to the very real dangers that lie ahead once we are equipped with the necessary information and documentation to convince our friends and loved ones of the disaster that may affect their jobs, their finances, and possibly their lives. In the balance of this book we will explore very practical strategies that you can follow to protect your family and home. We will also explore some strategies that will help minimize the dangers to your small business, church, or ministry from the Y2K crisis.

The book of 1 Chronicles in the Old Testament tells us that out of the twelve tribes of Israel, the tribe of Issachar was known for its wisdom and concern with "the times," or prophecy. "And of the children of Issachar, which were men that had understanding of the times, to know what Israel ought to do" (1 Chron. 12:32). This fascinating verse draws our attention to the fact that the men's knowledge and "understanding of the times" led directly to practical action; they knew "what Israel ought to do." The foreknowledge that you acquire about the Y2K crisis will benefit you and your loved ones. Remember, for those who trust in God, we are not alone in facing the crisis ahead. "Be strong and of a good courage, fear not, nor be afraid of them: for the Lord thy God, he it is that doth go with thee; he will not fail thee, nor forsake thee" (Deut. 31:6).

A Balanced View of the Duration of
Y2K Problems

It is also important that we understand the duration of the Y2K problem. First, while the worst effects may be triggered by computer failures in the first few days of January 2000, the computer experts warn that computer crashes and errors related to the inability to handle 2000 correctly have already begun crashing some systems and produced large errors. It is certain that computer crashes and failures will cause many problems in 1999, as well as in the year 2000 and 2001. However, to provide a proper balance to this overview, we need to keep in mind that this Y2K problem, although disruptive and expensive to correct, is a temporary problem. After a few months, or at worst a year, most of the systems will certainly be working again. Depending on the extent and duration of your city's (or county's) loss of power and phone utilities, banking system, and government's tax-collecting ability, the worst of the crisis could be over in a few months if you live in North America or Australia. However, for those who live in Europe, Asia, Africa, or South America, where little attention or work has been directed to fixing their computers, the duration of the breakdown might last one or two years. This could be devastating. It is impossible to be certain how badly any particular city or neighborhood may be affected by computer breakdowns, but all of the most cautious experts are extremely concerned. Therefore, I believe the most practical strategy is this: "Pray for the best—prepare for the worst!"

One of my strongest recommendations is that you find a small group of friends or family members who are equally interested in protecting themselves from the worst impact of this computer meltdown and begin meeting once a month or so as a study group. You will be able to exchange data as well as resources for information and equipment. Furthermore, such a group is likely to be of great help in keeping you focused on the need to take practical action rather than simply accumulate more information. The longer you wait to take action on some of the practical strategies I suggest in this book, the more likely that your delay may cost you in terms of equipment, financial losses, etc.

After you pass the denial stage and begin to appreciate the enormous risk to our economy and modern life from the Y2K disaster, it would be easy to let the staggering complexity of this computer catastrophe overwhelm you. We must realize that if we have faith in God, we are not alone. He has promised to guide our steps and to give us the needed wisdom to handle the challenges we will meet.

In the book of Proverbs the Lord commands us, "Trust in the Lord with all thine heart; and lean not unto thine own understanding. In all thy ways acknowledge him, and he shall direct thy paths" (3:5-6). Throughout my life, this verse, a favorite of my parents as well, has strengthened me innumerable times when I faced challenges and major decisions. "Fear thou not; for I am with thee: be not dismayed; for I am thy God: I will strengthen thee; yea, I will help thee; yea, I will uphold thee with the right hand of my righteousness" (Isa. 41:10).

As we explore a series of possible strategies for minimizing the dangers from Y2K, remember the Scripture's promise: "And the Lord shall guide thee continually, and satisfy thy soul in drought, and make fat thy bones: and thou shalt be like a watered garden, and like a spring of water, whose waters fail not" (Isa. 58:11).

Practical Strategies to Protect Against Y2K

Personal Records

Obtain the most recent paper records of your accounts.

One of the most significant strategies to protect yourself is to obtain printed records, during 1998 and 1999, of all of your most important personal and business records. If the relevant computer systems begin to produce errors or fail to function at all, these 1998 and 1999 hard-copy records will allow you to argue your case with the relevant corporation or government agency and resolve the issue in your favor. Without such records, you may find yourself at the mercy of the mistaken computer records of the agency or company that has been victimized by the Year 2000 computer virus.

These personal records should be maintained in your personal Year 2000 File and stored in a safe place. During the fall of 1999, it would be wise to obtain monthly records of the following items:

- Your banking records from your personal and corporate bank accounts
- Your insurance records from your automobile, fire, and life insurance company
- Your stock brokerage records from your broker
- Your passport records
- Your mutual fund account records
- Recent records of any additional investments
- Current records of tax payments on any real estate
- Your up-to-date mortgage statements from your mortgage company
- Your deeds and real estate records of every property you own
- A copy of your marriage records and birth certificates for each member of your family
- The last seven years of income tax records and filings by you,

your family, and your small business or ministry. In addition to your own photocopies, you can order an IRS copy by filing IRS Form 4506, which is called a "Request for Copy of Tax Form" from your local tax office. You would be wise to also request a copy of your state income tax returns for the last few years. For Canadians, you should request the equivalent federal tax forms from Revenue Canada, as well as the provincial tax return from your local provincial tax office.

- Your up-to-date Statement of Military Service records (Department of Defense Form 214 and Selective Service Records can be obtained from the National Personal Records Center, 9700 Page Blvd., St. Louis, MO 63132-5200)
- Your health/medical records from your doctor, health center, and hospital
- Records of loan payments and applications (student, VA, FHA, small business, etc.)
- Records from your various creditors showing your payments on your credit accounts for the last year
- A copy of your current credit records from your local credit-rating agency. The three largest credit reporting agencies in America that likely contain credit reports on you are the following: Equifax Credit Information Services, PO Box 740256, Atlanta, GA 30374; Experian National Consumer Assistance Center, PO Box 949, Allen, TX 75013-0949; and Trans Union, 760 Sproul Road, Springfield, PA 19064.
- A copy of your municipal tax records showing your last tax payments
- Any court records covering bankruptcy, trials, judgments, etc.
- A copy of your electrical, water, gas, and cable television account records
- A copy of your entitlements from the U.S. Social Security Administration or the Canadian Pension Plan regarding pension payments due to you or your spouse. For U.S. citizens, I strongly suggest that you obtain from the Social Security Administration an up-to-date Statement on Earnings and Benefits (request S.S.A. Form 7004). The national U.S. Social Security toll-free number is (800) 772-1213. Otherwise, you can call your local Social Security phone number, as listed in your local phone book. When you receive your Form 7004,

complete it and mail it back to Social Security; you will receive a Statement of Earnings and Benefits in two months. Keep this as an important part of your Year 2000 file. It would be wise to request an up-to-date Statement of Earnings and Benefits approximately every six months so you will have current records to validate your claim if the Social Security computers are hopelessly confused. Older American citizens that are already receiving Social Security benefit checks would be wise to photocopy their check or automatic deposit slips for future reference, in case there is any confusion in their computer records.

Educational Records

Write to the schools you attended and obtain a transcript of your academic records and degrees. If your alma mater loses some of its data in the computer crisis, you will be happy that you had the foresight to request a hard copy of those degrees and grades you invested so much time and money in obtaining.

Medical Records

If you or a member of your family has a complex medical problem, it would be very useful to have a complete personal copy of these records. In the event of computer disruptions, the loss of such records could make it difficult to verify insurance claims or to obtain proper medical treatment. However, I must warn you, based on personal research, it may be difficult to actually obtain such records. A registered letter to the head of the hospital or medical facility signed by your lawyer may provide the best chance of getting a copy of your medical records released.

Medical Emergencies

If you or a member of your family has serious medical problems that necessitate the regular taking of prescription medicine, it would be wise to discuss this matter with your family doctor and pharmacist. Computer problems affecting the manufacture or distribution of drugs or your pharmacy's prescription records could disrupt the availability of these vitally needed drugs and thus threaten your family's health at a time it would be wise to stay clear of the emergency wing of your local hospital. Many hospitals will experience severe computer breakdowns in 2000. You probably should suggest to your doctor that he write an emergency four-month supply of any essential prescription before the end of 1999. It would be wise to acquire an extra set of eyeglasses if they are essential.

Home Security Systems

Check with your home and office electronic security system management to verify reliability in the new millennium. Write to the president of your security company and ask for a written commitment that their company's security service is certified as Year 2000-compliant. Don't rely on any verbal commitments. Rely only on written commitments, and even then with caution.

Food Supplies

Consider the danger that the Y2K crisis may seriously disrupt the food distribution system on January 1, 2000. The situation may depend on the country you live in as well as the city. You should expect a certain amount of disruptions to the normal, error-free delivery of food to the millions of supermarkets, corner grocery stores, and restaurants. If your personal analysis of the Y2K problem suggests that your city may suffer from food-delivery disruptions, then you might consider acquiring a three or six-month supply of freeze-dried food and various canned foods that will be edible for six months or more. There are reliable suppliers of such products listed in the appendix.

A fundamental rule regarding food storage is "Store the food that you will eat and eat the food you store." In light of the fact that the average grocery store has only a three-day supply of food on its shelves, any Y2K computer breakdown of the railroad and trucking system will lead to severe disruption of food supplies. Therefore, a prudent person may consider whether or not a wise insurance policy might involve acquiring a supply of food that will allow your family to eat normally until regular food supplies return to the stores and restaurants.

The U.S. Department of Agriculture has produced a booklet

entitled *Family Food Stockpile For Survival* (Home and Garden Bulletin No. 77). The booklet advises:

> Safeguard your family's survival by planning your food and water stockpile now. . . Every family should either build up and keep a 2-week supply of regular food in the home at all times or assemble and maintain a special 2-week stockpile of survival foods. . . . Individuals and families are responsible for maintaining personal stocks of food and water in their homes . . . sufficient to meet their needs until other supplies are available.

It is relatively easy today for a person to acquire a supply of dehydrated, freeze-dried food, and bulk food supplies from local and national suppliers. The Y2K Resources section at the end of this book will give you a number of national suppliers that can provide catalogs offering numerous freeze-dried and bulk food supplies. I strongly recommend that anyone who believes that Y2K is a serious danger should write or phone to obtain catalogs and information that will allow you to make preparations to minimize the disruptions and inconveniences that will likely occur during the first few months of the year 2000. These resources can provide supplies of freeze-dried food in packages that will give you ample food for a single adult for durations from three days, one month, three months, and up to one year. To give you an idea of the possible costs, one supplier offers a one-month supply of freeze-dried food for approximately $350 and a one-year supply for less than $1000. A word to the wise: the manufacturing capacity of these emergency survival companies is very limited. If you delay too long you may find that it will be impossible to acquire these pre-packaged food packages because their limited manufacturing capacity will be quickly exhausted. Consider the purchase of a supply of canned food and other foods that will store well for a number of months and will supplement your supply of freeze-dried foods to provide variety in your diet during an emergency.

Consider acquiring special foods that you appreciate that will provide variety during an emergency. If you have the space in your property you might consider growing a garden in 1999 that will provide a number of vegetables to supplement your family's diet. Purchase a book on gardening that will tell you how to grow the best nutritious foods for your family. However, make certain that you avoid hybrid seeds that will not reproduce next year because they are sterile. Ask the supplier to be absolutely certain that the seeds you acquire for your garden are non-hybrid seeds that will grow vegetables and will produce additional seeds that you can re-plant the following year. Caution: do not buy seed grains for eating (they may have been treated with pesticides that will poison you). Make certain that the grains you buy for baking, etc. are the consumption grain seeds that are more expensive, but edible. Make certain that you also acquire the necessary amount of pet food to feed your dog or cat.

Water Supplies

While we can survive for a few days without food our bodies require water every day. It is strongly recommended that you obtain emergency water supplies equal to two gallons per day for drinking, cooking, cleaning, etc. for each person in your family for the duration of the expected emergency when your water service may be disrupted by Y2K electrical power outages. Obviously, no one can know precisely how long power might be unavailable in your area so you must prudently determine what amount of water storage is appropriate. At the very least every family should acquire one 55 gallon high-density water storage barrel that would hold enough water for two people for two weeks. Multiple 55 gallon barrels will provide inexpensive but possibly vital family protection. Remember to purchase a bung wrench to allow you to open and close the bung plugs on your storage barrels. An easily available alternative would be to rinse out large bottles of pop and then use the container to store an emergency water reserve. Add a few drops of clorox bleach and tightly seal the bottles. It might be a wise precaution to fill all available containers in your home with water on December 31, 1999, including all sinks and bathtubs.

If you suddenly realize that your water supply has been interrupted you can usually acquire up to 60 gallons of drinkable water from within your home by opening the spigot at the bottom of your hot water heater in the basement. Open a tap on the top floor and drain this water into safe containers. Portable water filters or water preparation tablets are essential to purify water from other sources than your tap. In an emergency all water from alternative sources should be purified through filters, purification tablets, or the use of clorox (8 drops per gallon) or iodine (12 drops per gallon) with an eye dropper. Another excellent purification product is Aerobic 07 which has no bad taste. A one-ounce bottle (approximately $12) will protect 55 gallons of water for five years.

Emergency Tools

The suppliers listed in the Y2K Resources section will offer ample tools that will prove helpful in any emergency. Since batteries may not be readily available, a good emergency kit will include regular batteries as well as solar-powered and hand-powered flashlights and radios that will enable you to receive important news broadcasts. A supply of long-burning candles, oil-burning lamps, and snap light sticks that provide reliable and safe light for 12 hours will be valuable in any future emergency. Fire-starting materials including waterproof matches, lighters, or a magnesium fire starter are essential. Solar-powered or hand-powered radios will be very useful because a reliable radio will be essential during any future emergency. As a long-time camper, I strongly recommend that you acquire a multi-tooled Swiss Army knife or equivalent as part of any emergency kit. The purchase of a convenient and safe portable stove that can be used for indoor or outdoor cooking that utilizes butane fuel cartridges will prove to be a very wise investment. A crowbar, saw, and axe will also prove helpful. Several industrial-strength fire extinguishers are critical to protect against fires.

Heating

One of the greatest concerns about the Y2K crisis is that it will affect the people living in northern areas of North America, Europe, and Russia during the coldest months of winter. The power utilities are still dangerously unprepared for the problems caused by their non-compliant mainframe computers and their thousands of embedded microchips. Therefore, a prudent reader may consider the advisability of acquiring an ample supply of several cords of high-quality hardwood that can be burned in your fireplace or a wood-burning stove to heat your whole home for up to three months until spring arrives. It would be wise to purchase this supply of essential firewood as early as possible in 1998 to allow it to properly dry before you might need to use it. Placing a sheet of aluminum foil or equivalent material at the back and sides of your fireplace will greatly increase the amount of radiated heat from your fireplace.

Even a short-term disruption of electrical power plants may result in government edicts that demand that everyone reduce the temperature in their homes (to 60 degrees, for example). If you don't already own high-quality heavy-duty sleeping bags for each member of your family you should consider purchasing these items. An emergency space blanket or sleeping bag which reflects up to 90 percent of body heat will conserve your body heat during an emergency when normal heat may not be available for a period of several months.

Medical Emergencies

If any member of your family needs medical or dental care, it might be wise to complete such treatment before the end of 1999. Check with suppliers such as those listed in the Y2K Resources section at the end of this book to find the supplies necessary to protect your family from the medical risks caused by disruptions of basic health services in early 2000. A well-stocked family first aid kit for your home (estimated cost $50.00) and another smaller first aid kit for your car (estimated cost $30.00) may prove to be an extremely worthwhile investment. It is advisable to arrange for someone in your family to attend a St. John's Ambulance first aid course or equivalent in your city to learn how to handle medical emergencies. A first aid book should be part of your preparedness plan.

Sanitation

The breakdown of society's infrastructure, including power, water, and sewage will endanger your health and that of your family. The loss of electrical power will naturally affect your water and sewage as well. The proper handling of waste will avoid the worst dangers to your family's health. Some of the most essential emergency supplies include a large quantity of heavy plastic garbage bags, ample amounts of toilet paper, paper towels, cleaning supplies, and soap. Special concentrated liquid soap is valuable in a convenient plastic squeeze bottle. Also, pre-moistened towelettes ($1 for ten) will be valuable for cleansing without utilizing your precious drinking water. It is essential that everyone clean their hands properly to avoid transmitting dangerous germs.

Portable chemical toilets will prove helpful if the disruption continues for more than a few days. Carefully dispose of waste within sealed garbage bags inside sealed plastic containers. Permanently dispose of waste and garbage by burying it in a deep trench in your backyard as far as possible from the house. Cover the buried waste with the ashes from your fireplace (which contain lye) and a layer of earth. Alternatively you might buy a container of lye for this purpose. Adequate supplies of diapers and feminine sanitation products should be considered if necessary.

Electrical Power

If your analysis of your own local situation suggests that your area may experience sporadic or longer term disruptions of electrical power, you might consider acquiring a gasoline-powered electrical power generator to provide temporary electrical power. Those who live in states or provinces that are especially dependent upon nuclear power generating stations are extremely vulnerable to the Year 2000 problem. The nuclear regulating authorities may close down such systems out of concern for possible Three Mile Island or Chernobyl nuclear plant situations developing as a result of uncorrected Y2K problems. For example, a number of states in the Northeast United States receive as much as 50 percent of their electrical power from nuclear generating plants.

Fuel for heating and for cooking food for a short period of time may be advisable. Citizens living in such critical areas should seriously consider the possible impact on their family or business of prolonged electrical power brownouts or blackouts during the initial months of the new century. Although temporary in nature, the loss of electrical power may produce many problems for both families and businesses because the problems will occur during the coldest months of the years for those living in North America, Europe, Russia, and Japan. While it is quite possible to acquire a portable electrical generator in 1998, it may become increasingly expensive and more difficult to acquire such a generator in 1999, at any price, when the extent of the Year 2000 problem becomes apparent to the general public.

A word to the wise regarding electrical generators: If you decide to pursue this option I highly recommend that you hire a competent professional to assist you. First, the small electrical generators used by campers are usually insufficiently powerful to provide the electricity for a home. Therefore, if you choose this option you will probably need to acquire a larger electrical generator such as would be used on a farm, though this will be rather expensive. In addition, the fuel supply for your generator must be safely stored on your property. If you live in a city or town it may be impossible to store a significant amount of fuel safely and legally. When a generator produces more power than what is needed immediately it may be necessary to utilize expensive and bulky storage batteries. An electronic controller is required to handle the charging and discharging cycles as well as the purchase of an electrical inverter to convert the direct current (DC) produced by your generator into the alternating current (AC) that you need to power the lights, heating, etc. in your home. Another possible option is to consider acquiring a solar-powered generator which will eliminate the problems of fuel storage. Depending on the amount of sunshine available in your state or province, this may be an attractive choice.

Bartering

In the potential economic chaos that may follow the breakdown of many of our essential infrastructure systems following January 1, 2000, the banking system may be disrupted for a period of time in parts of the country. If this situation develops, your ability to barter and trade quality and desirable items for other supplies that your family needs will prove to be extremely valuable. If the local banks are in disarray because of Y2K problems it may be very important that you have valuable items to barter with your neighbors to acquire the items that you have not purchased before the crisis began. In light of this reality, to the extent that your financial resources permit, I would recommend that you consider purchasing ample quantities of all of the listed survival items because they will prove to be extremely valuable for bartering at a time that most of those around you will find themselves woefully unprepared.

Financial Matters

Avoid the use of a safe deposit box in a bank to hold your cash. You may not have immediate access to your needed funds if the bank folds or is temporarily closed under the Monetary Control Act of 1980. Consider using a safety deposit storage company.

Place some of your funds in a number of solid banks, making certain that you keep less than the Federal Deposit Insurance Corporation insured limit. While the FDIC does insure U.S. bank deposits in member banks up to the limit of $100,000 per depositor, it is important that you remember that the $100,000 limit applies to the depositor, not to the individual accounts. In other words, if you have $150,000 in several different accounts within an insured bank that fails, the FDIC will only insure your total deposits to the maximum of $100,000. Therefore, diversify your investments and place your savings funds in a variety of strong banks keeping the total amount *in each bank* at less than $100,000. In Canada, the federal deposit insurance only protects your account up to the limit of $60,000. Therefore, a Canadian would be well advised to diversify his investment savings accounts at Canadian banks by placing no more than $60,000 in any particular bank. Look for ads that declare that a bank is Year 2000-compliant.

It will be imperative that you have significant amounts of your money available in cash in the months before and after January 1, 2000. Long before that date we are likely to see the beginnings of panicked runs on the bank in various countries (such as Japan) that could easily lead to a chain reaction throughout the world. Many financial advisors believe that it may begin first in Asia, where Japanese housewives tend to control the large amounts of family savings. Many Japanese save as much as thirty percent of their household income each year. As soon as they become aware of the significant chance that their banks may not be able to survive the Y2K crisis, the bank runs may begin.

Removing your life savings and mutual funds quietly in the months before the bank panic begins may be prudent. Should you remove only some of your funds or all of them? The decision is obviously yours alone. You need to carefully consider the risk versus the loss of interest or appreciation that your invested funds would hopefully earn if they remained fully invested through the balance of 1998 and 1999. If you seriously doubt that there is a real danger to your funds from the Year 2000 computer bug, you might choose to continue investing your funds exactly where they are. However, if you feel that the risks of a severe stock market correction are very strong, you may choose to remove your investments from the stock market as the Year 2000 deadline approaches.

Investments

Where should you place your investment funds? First of all, gather all of your investment records and analyze them from the standpoint of their risk in light of the Y2K problem. If you assess the risk to your funds invested directly in the stock market or indirectly within a mutual fund as high, you might choose to withdraw those funds and invest them in more conservative investments (such as federal government savings bonds, Treasury bills, or the investment certificates of a major bank if you are absolutely convinced that the particular bank is Year 2000-compliant).

An interim place to park your funds between now and the summer of 1999 might be in a solid money market account with a well-known broker that invests in safe federal government securities such as T-bills. However, as the banking crisis begins to impact our economy, you may want to have your life savings and investment funds transformed into real cash. At that point, you might withdraw your cash from your stock broker, mutual fund, bank, or ATM machine over a period of several weeks or months. You might consider placing these funds in a secure fireproof safe or in a safety deposit box in a safety deposit storage company.

A word to the wise: Do not talk to anyone but your spouse or children about your plans. Advise them to treat the matter of your personal preparations for food reserves, etc., as a family secret.

16

Practical Y2K Strategies for Small Businesses and Ministries

The Challenge

Whether you are running a small business or managing a ministry, the Year 2000 computer crisis will prove to be one of the greatest challenges you likely will ever face. The special dangers associated with Y2K can seem almost overwhelming. Almost every area of your organization, from your suppliers and service providers to your customers or clients, are equally at risk. In this chapter I will outline a checklist of practical strategies and actions that will minimize the damage to your organization from this crisis.

The possible loss of electrical power for a period of hours, days, or weeks would be devastating to business or ministry. Depending on the location of your business or ministry, you might experience serious power shortages for some period of time. Brownouts and occasional blackouts are possible, depending on your location. Organizations in Europe, Asia, South America, and Africa (where work on Y2K problems has only just begun) may suffer from longer power outages. Computer systems do not react well to power surges, spikes, or failures. Often computer data can be lost or corrupted. Companies might consider acquiring power-interruption equipment that will protect computers in the case of power outages, giving the company the time to safely shut down the system. Other companies may consider whether a gas or diesel-fueled electrical generator would be practical to keep their equipment functioning.

The business world is extremely vulnerable from the multitude of other systems that may experience crashes, in addition to their mainframe and desktop computers. For example, many Private Branch Exchange (PBX) phone systems have noncompliant embedded microchips that may cause the system to fail. Obviously, most businesses could barely operate if the telephone system experiences Y2K problems. This problem could potentially impair voice, fax, teletype, and computer modem communications. The good news is that tests suggest that the Internet itself is likely to keep functioning properly. However, if the Internet remained one of the only reliable methods of communication, the overwhelming usage might slow the system considerably. Corporations may have to depend increasingly on the post office and courier services in the initial months of the Year 2000. However, both of these systems are also vulnerable to Y2K problems.

Corporations should discuss this crisis with the manufacturers of their computers, security systems, elevators, faxes, phones, heating and air-conditioning equipment. Obtain written confirmation that they are Y2K-compliant.

If the banks in your country or city experience severe problems in the first few months of 2000, companies may find it impossible to pay their employees. In anticipation of this, some companies may choose to withdraw a significant amount of cash from their bank accounts in late 1999 to enable them to compensate employees in cash until the crisis passes. However, if many firms choose this course of action, the banks could quickly find themselves running out of paper currency. Unfortunately, business-interruption insurance policies are unlikely to provide any coverage for Y2K problems because the policies only cover "unforeseen" contingencies. It would be hard to argue that the year 2000 was an unforeseen event. Additionally, most insurance companies are now introducing clauses in their renewal policies that specifically exclude Year 2000 computer problems.

Every business depends on a great number of other corporations as suppliers, service providers, and customers. It is essential that businesses carefully analyze their vulnerability to Y2K problems experienced by these other businesses. If a company's present bank is noncompliant, it would be prudent to develop a relationship with a new bank that is Y2K ready. Some corporations are establishing accounts with several banks to give them additional options if one bank fails to provide reliable service. Many businesses are now communicating with their suppliers, service providers, and customers and asking them to certify whether or not they are 2000-compliant. It is important to receive this confirmation in writing on the company's letterhead and signed by a corporate officer. Verbal assurances that "all is well" or that they are "working on it" are of no value. At the end of this chapter is a sample letter that a business owner might send to other companies to verify their readiness to operate reliably in the next century.

A Checklist of Practical Strategies

1) Complete an inventory of the equipment you use in your office or plant.

2) In 1999, send a letter of inquiry to each manufacturer asking if they will guarantee that the equipment in question will operate normally on January 1, 2000. There is little point in requesting such information about Y2K compliance until 1999 because most computer modifications will not be completed and tested until some time in 1999, at best.

3) Check with key suppliers to verify that their products and operations are compliant.

4) Check for Y2K compliance before purchasing any additional computers or equipment.

5) Write to your bank and request a written response as to their Y2K compliance.

6) If you remain in doubt about your bank's compliance, consider setting up a second business bank account with another bank in your community that is Y2K-compliant.

7) Verify that all of your communications systems are compliant, especially your PBX, voice mail, fax, modems, and office phone system.

8) Complete an inventory of all computers used in your operations and verify that they are Y2K-compliant. If not, repair or replace noncompliant hardware. Be very careful of testing your computer's Y2K compliance by setting the system clock to January 1, 2000. Some commercial software has a time limit of a certain number of years under your software license agreement. In some cases, resetting the computer's system clock to 2000 may cause the application to conclude that the license has expired (check with your network supervisor).

9) Complete an inventory of all computer software applications, including your computer's operating system, to verify that the essential programs are Y2K-compliant. Replace or upgrade all noncompliant software.

10) Carefully check for any customized software, such as spreadsheets, databases, etc., that may be noncompliant due to the nearly universal practice of recording dates using only two digits.

11) Write to the utility companies that supply your electrical power, water, sewage, etc., and ask for a written response confirming their readiness to function reliably in the year 2000. Some utility consultants suggest it might be prudent to disconnect your equipment from the power outlets over the New Year's Eve weekend to avoid any possible dangers from power interruptions or surges.

12) Consider the purchase of a high-quality surge protector to protect your equipment from surges and spikes in the electrical power due to Y2K problems. Power-interruption equipment can protect your computers against damage to data from unexpected power shortages, which are possible in the year 2000.

13) Check with the management of your office building as to their Y2K preparations to make certain that the building's computerized security system and other critical systems are Y2K-compliant.

14) Create a backup copy of every important computer record and program in your organization and keep it on removable media

(such as a JAZ or ZIP drive cartridge). If your computer should crash or hopelessly corrupt your data files, a clean backup copy will be essential.

15) Avoid any unnecessary business travel by plane or train in the first few weeks of 2000.

16) Advise your accounting staff to carefully scrutinize all invoices and statements in 1999 and 2000, especially if a date appears as "00." Look for gross errors, such as statements that claim you owe ninety-nine years of interest charges or penalties on a past-due bill.

17) Be especially vigilant with your accountants regarding personal and corporate income tax filings and refunds in 2000.

18) Obtain hard-copy records of all important financial records, such as financial statements from your bank, insurance payments, pension records, tax payments, utility bills, etc.

19) In late 1999, consider acquiring a current copy of your personal and corporate credit reports from the major credit reporting agencies to make certain that Y2K accounting errors will not produce inaccurate negative credit reports.

A Sample Letter of Y2K Inquiry

Date
Company Name
Address

Re: Year 2000 Computer Crisis

Dear Sir,

I am a customer of your company and have placed my business with your firm for several years. After completing some research on the Year 2000 computer crisis (sometimes called Y2K), I am very concerned that this problem may interfere with the ability of many companies to operate reliably in the first few months of the next century.

After December 31, 1999, computer software that uses two digits to identify the year may misinterpret "00" to be 1900 rather than 2000. Computers that are not corrected in time may either shut down or produce miscalculations regarding dates. Almost every business and government agency throughout the world is at risk of disruption unless every system is fixed before January 1, 2000.

Some experts have calculated that the total costs to fix all of the computers throughout the world may exceed $600 billion. However, the ultimate costs of failing to correct these computer systems could be even more expensive. Failure to meet the deadline may result in the government being unable to collect taxes, pay its employees, or make pension payments. If some banks, insurance companies, or other financial institutions don't correct their computers in time, it may be impossible for their business customers to make purchases or produce their payroll. There is serious danger of widespread disruptions to essential infrastructure, including electric power, water, telephones, and even heating systems. The evidence is overwhelming that the Year 2000 computer crisis is the greatest technological challenge that the business world and governments have ever faced.

In light of this crisis and because of the reliance I have placed in your company, I request that you confirm to me in writing that your business is taking strong action to fix your computer systems to insure that you will continue to provide reliable service and products after January 1, 2000. I would appreciate your answering this letter as soon as possible.

Yours Sincerely,

17

Implications and Decisions: The Good News

There is strong evidence that our modern industrialized world will experience a crisis as we enter the next millennium. My purpose in writing this book has been to awaken you to the nature and magnitude of this crisis and to help you make practical preparations for the protection of your family. I hope that the information and strategies that I have suggested will also assist owners of small businesses and ministries in minimizing the risk of severe disruption to their organizations. During the last few months I have noted a growing awareness of the approaching Y2K catastrophe and the onset of real fear in the minds of many as they realize the potential this computer meltdown has to damage jobs and finances.

I trust that the balanced and well-documented information presented in *The Millennium Meltdown* will prepare you both mentally and spiritually for the difficulties that lie ahead. I am not a prophet; I cannot predict precisely how Y2K will impact your job, family, or finances. The dangers are real, but the devastation caused by this computer crisis will vary widely, depending upon the country and state that you live in, the degree of Year 2000 readiness of your government and local banks, and most of all, whether or not your region loses electrical power for a period of time.

Developing a Proper Perspective on the Year 2000 Crisis

Although the Year 2000 crisis will certainly be the largest and most expensive technology disaster in history, in all likelihood the worst effects will only last a few months to a year. Even if the banks in your area close and the government's services are interrupted for a few weeks or months, these services will be restored eventually. The key principle that should guide your preparation is to take action now. We must trust in God to give us the wisdom to understand this complex situation and to make the right decisions. It would be easy to let this crisis overwhelm us to the point that we become paralyzed with fear.

However, *The Millennium Meltdown* has suggested practical strategies that you can follow in the months ahead that will make an enormous difference to the quality of your life when the computers begin to fail. Those who are forewarned about the dangers of the coming crisis will be forearmed to protect themselves and their friends. Practical preparations made today will make a tremendous difference in the first few months of the year 2000.

The apostle Paul reminds us, "For God hath not given us the spirit of fear; but of power, and of love, and of a sound mind" (2 Tim. 1:7). Those who have a personal relationship with Jesus Christ can trust in Him to give them "a sound mind" as they make preparations to meet this unique millennial challenge. King David declared his faith in the Lord to guide and provide for him in these words: "This poor man cried, and the Lord heard him, and saved him out of all his troubles. The angel of the Lord encampeth round about them that fear him, and delivereth them. O taste and see that the Lord is good: blessed is the man that trusteth in him. O fear the Lord, ye his saints: for there is no want to them that fear him" (Ps. 34:6-9). King David experienced a life filled with disasters, challenges, and triumphs. He also taught us to trust in God's mercy and provision. David wrote, "I have been young, and now am old; yet have I not seen the righteous forsaken, nor his seed begging bread" (Ps. 37:25).

However, if you have never trusted Jesus Christ as your personal Lord and Savior, you need to carefully consider the issue at hand. The Bible makes it clear that every one of us must decide whom we will follow. Who will be the god of your life? Either you admit you are a sinner, in need of pardon, and accept Jesus as your Lord, or you insist on leading your own path and essentially remaining your own god. If you insist on being your own god, you may succeed in this life, yet you will face an eternity spent in hell. The Scriptures warn us that pride is the greatest sin. Our pride is revealed in our stubborn attitudes of independence from God, as we so often choose our own direction. Milton spoke of this fundamental choice in his epic poem *Paradise Lost*. He wrote that in the end either we will say to God, "Thy will be done" or God will say to us, "Thy will be done."

Ultimately, it is your choice. You must choose heaven or hell as your eternal destiny. If you choose to commit your life to Jesus Christ, you will meet Him at the Resurrection as your Savior. If you choose to reject Him, you will have chosen to meet Him at the Resurrection as your final judge. The Lord through the apostle Paul echoes his pronouncement in Isaiah in declaring that one day "every knee shall bow to me, and every tongue shall confess to God" (Rom. 14:11; Isa. 45:23).

The author of Hebrews said, "It is appointed unto men once to die, but after this the judgment" (Heb. 9:27). God warns, "For all have sinned, and come short of the glory of God" (Rom. 3:23). In light of the many prophetic signs that point to His near return, including the rush toward world government and a cashless society, each of us must make our choice. Every day sin leads men and women inexorably toward hell and an eternity without God. "For the wages of sin is death; but the gift of God is eternal life through Jesus Christ our Lord" (Rom. 6:23). However, God loves us so much that He sent His Son Jesus to suffer the punishment for our sins, for any who confess their sin and ask for forgiveness. In the Gospel of John, the prophet declared, "But as many as received him, to them gave he power to become the sons of God, even to them that believe on his name" (John 1:12).

The only basis upon which you will be allowed to enter heaven will be your relationship to Jesus Christ. God demands perfect holiness and righteousness. Therefore, since we are all sinners, no one has the right to enter heaven on their own merits. It is impossible for a Holy God to allow an unrepentant sinner into a sinless heaven. Since God cannot ignore the fact that we have all sinned against Him, it was necessary that someone who was perfectly sinless should pay the penalty of physical and spiritual death, as a substitute. The only person who qualified was Jesus Christ, the Holy Son of God.

Christ's sacrificial gift paid the full price for our sins. By accepting His pardon, we are able to stand before the Judgment Seat of God, clothed in Christ's righteousness: "For he hath made him [Jesus] to be sin for us, who knew no sin; that we might be made the righteousness of God in Him" (2 Cor. 5:21). Jesus Christ's atonement for our sins is perhaps the greatest mystery in creation. He loves each of us so much that He chose to die upon that cross to secure our salvation.

Nicodemus, a righteous religious leader in ancient Israel, listened to Christ's teaching one night as he visited Him in secret. He asked Jesus about salvation. Jesus answered in these words, "Verily, verily, I say unto thee, Except a man be born again, he cannot see the kingdom of God" (John 3:3). Jesus explained to him, "Except a man be born of water and of the Spirit, he cannot enter into the kingdom of God" (John 3:5). It isn't enough that you intellectually accept the historical truth about Christ. To be born again you must sincerely repent of your sinful life, ask Christ to forgive you, and wholeheartedly place your trust in Him. This decision will transform your life. God will give you new purpose and meaning. The Lord promises believers eternal life in heaven: "This is the will of him who sent me, that everyone who sees the Son and believes in him may have everlasting life; and I will raise him up at the last day" (John 6:40). The moment you commit to Christ, you will receive eternal life. Though someday our bodies will die, we will live forever with Christ in heaven. Jesus explained to Nicodemus, "For God so loved the world, that he gave his only begotten Son, that whosoever believeth in him should not perish, but have everlasting life" (John 3:16). Jesus challenges you to consider your choice in terms of eternity, "For what shall it profit a man, if he shall gain the whole world, and lose his own soul?" (Mark 8:36).

If you are already a follower of Jesus Christ, consider sharing

The Millennium Meltdown with your friends and family, not only to awaken them to the coming computer crisis, but also to share your faith in Him. Our awareness of the nearness of the return of Jesus, in light of the fulfillment of the prophecies of the rise of a world government, should rekindle our love of Christ and our passion to witness to those around us while there is still time.

The incredible events in the coming months, as the Year 2000 computer crisis impacts our society, will cause many to question what lies ahead for the world. There is a growing fascination with the prophecies of the Bible regarding the events that will transpire in the last days. The tremendous interest and concern of our fellow citizens with the approaching Y2K crisis provides us with a tremendous opportunity to share practical strategies of preparation as well as to share our faith in Jesus Christ—our ultimate security in an uncertain world.

Selected Bibliography and Resource Material

de Jager, Peter and Richard Bergeon. *Managing '00: Surviving the Year 2000 Computing Crisis.* New York: John Wiley & Sons, 1997.

Feiler, Jesse and Barbara Butler. *Finding and Fixing Your Year 2000 Problem.* New York: AP Professional, 1997.

Fletcher, Michael W. *Computer Crisis 2000.* Washington: Self Counsel Press, 1998.

Hyatt, Michael S. *The Millennium Bug.* Washington: Regnery Publishing Inc., 1998.

Jones, Capers. *The Year 2000 Software Problem.* New York: Addison-Wesley, 1998.

Jones, Keith. *Year 2000 Software Crisis.* New York: International Thomson Computer Press, 1997.

Keogh, Jim. *Solving The Year 2000 Problem.* New York: AP Professional, 1997.

O'Connor, Patrick. *You Are The Target - Don't Be The Victim.* Phone: 44 1705 631751.

Lord, Jim. *A Survival Guide For the Year 2000 Problem.* Bowie: J J Marion Publishing, 1997.

Miller, Stewart S. *Year 2000 Solutions: A Manager's Guide to the Impending Collapse of Every IT System.* Springer Verlag, 1997.

Murray, Jerome T. and Marilyn Murray. *The Year 2000 Computer Crisis.* New York: McGraw-Hill Publishing, 1996.

Ragland, Bryce. *The Year 2000 Problem Solver.* New York: McGraw-Hill Publishing, 1997.

Reeve, Simon and Colin McGhee. *The Millennium Bug.* London: Vison Paperbacks, 1996.

Ulrich, William M. and Ian S. Hayes. *The Year 2000 Software Crisis.* Upper Saddle River: Yourdon Press, 1997.

Yourdon, Edward and Jennifer Yourdon. *Time Bomb 2000.* Upper Saddle River: Prentice Hall, 1998.

Yourdon, Edward and Jennifer Yourdon. *Time Bomb 2000: What the Year 2000 Computer Crisis Means to You!* London: Prentice Hall, 1998.

Notice from the publisher regarding
The Millennium Meltdown

The Millennium Meltdown offers only general observations based on the author's research, and makes no specific recommendations.

Our intention in this book is to provide Grant Jeffrey's opinions regarding economic and practical implications of the approaching Year 2000 computer crisis. Neither Frontier Research Publications, Inc. nor Grant Jeffrey is able to provide individual advice. Frontier Research and the author are not engaged in rendering legal, accounting, investing, or other professional advice. The reader should seek the services of a qualified professional accountant, lawyer, or financial planner before taking any actions.

The author and the publisher cannot be held responsible for any loss incurred as a result of the application of any of the information in this book. We have endeavored to assure the accuracy of the statistics and information that appear throughout this book. Please remember that *The Millennium Meltdown* is a guide, not a definitive source of investment information. When you have a specific question about your individual situation, check with your accountant, broker, banker, or financial consultant.

Reasons Why Some People Don't Worry About the Year 2000 Crisis

One of the greatest reasons for the almost universal procrastination regarding the unprecedented Year 2000 computer crisis is that we all have a natural tendency to deny that anything could threaten our normal way of life and our financial well-being. Almost everyone who has studied this crisis began their research in a state of denial. However, after a period of time, every serious researcher has come to the conclusion that we are truly facing the greatest challenge in our lives.

As you share the information in this book with your friends and family you will often hear disbelieving comments such as those listed below. As the news media belatedly awakens to the coming catastrophe during the next few months, the people around you will gradually begin to realize that this crisis is genuine. The information in this book should prepare you for the approaching crisis as well as enable you to help those around you during the first few months of the year 2000.

Check off the comments you have heard about Y2K

- [ ] Bill Gates and Microsoft will solve it.
- [ ] I think someone else must be working on this.
- [ ] If Y2K was real, surely President Clinton and Al Gore would have warned us years ago.
- [ ] I expect my company to be bankrupt long before the deadline.
- [ ] Hollywood movies reveal that a miraculous solution can always be found in the last 5 minutes.
- [ ] The tabloid newspapers reveal that the world will be destroyed before A.D. 2000.
- [ ] A newspaper article said that Y2K is simply hype to sell books and employ consultants.
- [ ] We can live without computers, can't we?
- [ ] Is there a Year 2000 problem?
- [ ] So far we haven't seen the Millennium bug. When it shows up we plan to spray it!

A Sample Letter of Y2K Inquiry

Consider sending a copy of this letter to any of the banks, insurance companies, landlords, or other significant suppliers of goods and services that are essential to your lifestyle.

Date
Name
Address

Re: **Year 2000 Computer Crisis**

Dear Sir,

I am a customer of your company and have placed my business with your firm for several years. After completing some research on the Year 2000 Computer Crisis (sometimes called Y2K), I am very concerned that this problem may interfere with the ability of many companies to operate reliably in the first few months of the next century.

After December 31, 1999, computer software that uses two digits to identify the year may misinterpret "00" to be 1900, rather than 2000. Computers that are not corrected in time may either shut down or provide wrong calculations regarding dates. Virtually every business and government agency throughout the world is at risk of disruption, unless every system is fixed before January 1, 2000.

Some experts have calculated that the total costs to fix all of the computers, throughout the world, may exceed $600 billion. However, the ultimate costs of failing to correct these computer systems could be even more expensive. Failure to meet the deadline may result in the government being unable to collect taxes, pay its employees, or make pension payments. If some banks, insurance companies, or other financial institutions don't correct their computers in time, it may be impossible for their business customers to make purchases or produce their payroll. There is serious danger of widespread disruptions to essential infrastructure, including electric power; water; telephones; and even heating systems. The evidence is overwhelming that the Year 2000 computer crisis is the greatest technological challenge that the business world and government have ever faced.

In light of this crisis and because of the reliance I have placed in your company, I request that you confirm to me in writing that your business is taking strong action to fix your computer systems, to insure that you will continue to provide reliable service and products after January 1, 2000. I would appreciate your answering this letter as soon as possible.

Yours Sincerely,

Selected Resource Materials to Prepare for the Year 2000 Crisis

I highly recommend that you consider contacting some of the resources that I have listed below. After carefully examining their catalogues I believe that these firms offer excellent sources of survival supplies as well as freeze-dried food supplies. Obviously, there are many other excellent companies that you can find in your local phone book, but this list will give you a place to start. I have no business relationship with any of these companies.

Gold and Silver

Gold and silver coins are the best way to own precious metals. Gold bullion is less spendable and might be too expensive to purchase conveniently. In the event of financial chaos, these coins may prove to be very helpful. Always take physical possession of these coins.

USA: International Collectors Associates, Phoenix, AZ (800) 525-9556

Canada: Canadians can purchase gold coins or bullion from any of the five major banks.

Freeze Dried Food Reserves

With less than seventy-two hours of food supplies in most cities, our food distribution system is very vulnerable if there are computer errors and crashes in the first months of the Year 2000. Only you can decide if freeze-dried food reserves should be part of your Year 2000 plan. You need to decide whether you should provide emergency food for family members for a period of weeks, months, or, in the worst contingency, a year.

AlpineAire Foods — Gourmet Reserves, Box 926, Nevada, CA 95959, (800) 322-6325, Fax (530) 272-2624

Homestead Foods, 334 Meadowood Lane, Victor, MT 59875, (800) 838-3132

International Collectors Associates, Phoenix, AZ, (800) 525-9556

Nitro-PaK Preparedness Centre, 151 N. Main St., Heber City, Utah 84032, (800) 866-4876, Fax (801) 654-3860

Preparedness Resources, 3999 S. Main, Suite S-2, Salt Lake City, Utah 84107, (801) 268-3913, Ext. 125.

Ready Reserve Foods, 1442 S. Gage St., San Bernardino, CA 92408, (800) 453-2202, Fax (909) 796-2196

The Survival Center, Box 234, McKenna, WA 98558, (800) 321-2900

General Emergency Survival Resources

The disruptions in the early months of 2000 may necessitate various emergency supplies including portable chemical toilets, batteries, long burning candles, flashlights, first-aid kits, water treatment tablets, insulated clothing, etc. However, even if the world survives the beginning of the new millennium without major disruptions, the growing number of earthquakes, tornadoes, floods, and other hazards provides strong motivation for any prudent person to take action to protect their family from the possibility of a future disaster. Whether or not Y2K proves to be as disruptive as the worst predictions suggest, the growing number of disasters that occur daily throughout the world make it advisable for every prudent person to spend a certain amount of time and money to provide a minimal level of disaster protection.

The following list of companies represent a few of the suppliers that I have examined and believe are reliable suppliers for emergency equipment and food.

The Survival Center, Box 234, McKenna, WA 98558, (800) 321-2900

Sam Andy Emergency Supplies, Box 141741, Irving, TX 75014, (800) 331-0358

Major Army Navy Surplus, 435 W. Alondra Bl., Gardena, CA 90248, (800) 441-8855, Fax (310) 324-6909

Nitro-PaK Preparedness Centre, 151 N. Main St., Heber City, Utah 84032, (800) 866-4876, Fax (801) 654-3860

Cabela's Catalog, 1 Cabela Drive, Sidney, NE 69160, (800) 237-4444, Fax (800) 496-6329

The Optimum Preparedness Center, 106 Yelm Ave.W., Box 1979, Yelm, WA 98597, (360) 458-4602

Lehman's Non-Electric catalog, P.O. Box 41, Kidron, OH 44636, (330) 857-5757

Recommended Y2K Reading

One of the first things you should do regarding Y2K preparations is to acquire and read survival manuals that cover this subject in depth. I would recommend these resource books:

Time Bomb 2000. Edward and Jennifer Yourdon, Upper Saddle River, NJ: Prentice Hall, 1998.

Family Preparedness Handbook. James T. Stevens, 15123 Little Wren Lane, San Antonio, TX 78255, (210) 695-5108.

Guide to Emergency Survival Communications. Dave Ingram, Universal Electronics, Inc. 4555 Groves Rd., Ste. 12, Columbus, OH 43232, (614) 866-4605.

Emergency Survival Handbook. Optimum Preparedness Center, (360) 458-4602.

Making the Best of Basics. James T. Stevens, Optimum Preparedness Center, (360) 458-4602.

How To Hide Anything. Michael Connor, Paladin Press.

Basic Preparedness. The Survival Center, Box 234, McKenna, WA 98558, (800) 321-2900.

Recommended Magazines

Remnant Review (Dr. Gary North). 1217 St. Paul St., Baltimore, MD 21202, (410) 234-0691.

The McAlvany Intelligence Advisor (Don McAlvany) Box 84904, Phoenix, AZ 85071, (800) 528-0559.

Y2K Internet Web Sites Information Resources

http://www.Year2000@garynorth.com
  Dr. Gary North's site—the best Y2K web site

http://www.y2ktimebomb.com
  Westergaard 2000 Online, Dr. Edward Yardeni

http://www.SurviveY2K.com
  Jim Lord's site on Y2K preparations

http://www.rufftimes.com
  Howard Ruff—practical Y2K preparations

http://www.year2000.com/y2karticles.html
  Current Internet articles about Y2K

http://www.year2000.com/y2kdoomsday.html
  An overview of the Y2K crisis

http://www.bug2000.co.uk/index2.html
  A UK government Y2K site